W9-COH-700

Getting Ready to Drive

Other titles in the series **Life—A How-to Guide**

Dealing With Stress
A How-to Guide
Library ed. 978-0-7660-3439-6
Paperback 978-1-59845-309-6

Choosing a Community Service Career
A How-to Guide
Library ed. 978-1-59845-147-4
Paperback 978-1-59845-312-6

Friendship
A How-to Guide
Library ed. 978-0-7660-3442-6
Paperback 978-1-59845-315-7

Getting the Hang of Fashion and Dress Codes
A How-to Guide
Library ed. 978-0-7660-3444-0
Paperback 978-1-59845-313-3

Using Technology
A How-to Guide
Library ed. 978-0-7660-3441-9
Paperback 978-1-59845-311-9

Volunteering
A How-to Guide
Library ed. 978-0-7660-3440-2
Paperback 978-1-59845-310-2

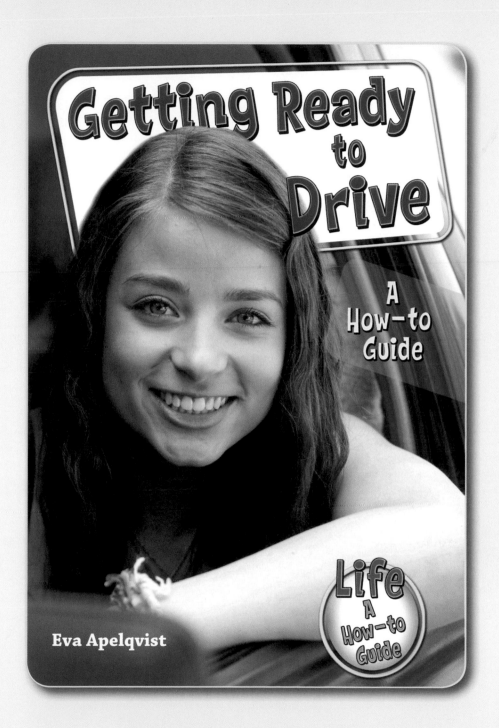

Getting Ready to Drive

A How-to Guide

Eva Apelqvist

Life
A How-to Guide

Enslow Publishers, Inc.
40 Industrial Road
Box 398
Berkeley Heights, NJ 07922
USA

http://www.enslow.com

For Sofia and Joakim, and safe, joyful driving

Library of Congress Cataloging-in-Publication Data
Apelqvist, Eva.
  Getting ready to drive : a how-to guide / Eva Apelqvist.
    p. cm.—(Life—a how-to guide)
  Includes bibliographical references and index.
  Summary: "Readers will learn about the general requirements for permits, driver's tests, different kinds of licenses, learning to drive, dangerous behavior, and other areas related to driving"—Provided by publisher.
  ISBN 978-0-7660-3443-3
  1. Automobile driving—Juvenile literature. I. Title.
  TL152.5.A64 2011
  629.28'3—dc22
                        2010016945

Paperback ISBN: 978-1-59845-314-0

062011 Lake Book Manufacturing, Inc., Melrose Park, IL

Printed in the United States of America

10 9 8 7 6 5 4 3 2 1

To Our Readers: We have done our best to make sure all Internet addresses in this book were active and appropriate when we went to press. However, the author and the publisher have no control over and assume no liability for the material available on those Internet sites or on other Web sites they may link to. Any comments or suggestions can be sent by e-mail to comments@enslow.com or to the address on the back cover.

Every effort has been made to locate all copyright holders of material used in this book. If any errors or omissions have occurred, corrections will be made in future editions of this book.

♻ Enslow Publishers, Inc., is committed to printing our books on recycled paper. The paper in every book contains 10% to 30% post-consumer waste (PCW). The cover board on the outside of each book contains 100% PCW. Our goal is to do our part to help young people and the environment too!

Illustration Credits: © Blend Images RF/Photolibrary, p. 35; © Christine Glade/iStock-photo.com, p. 6; © Gene Chutka/iStockphoto.com, p. 31; © Gunter Marx/Alamy, p. 49; Alan Hoffring/National Cancer Institute, p. 10; Pennsylvania Driver & Vehicle Services, p. 25; © 2011 Photos.com, a division of Getty Images. All rights reserved., pp. 18, 45, 53, 79, 92; Shutterstock.com, pp. 1, 5, 13, 27, 40, 42, 58, 61, 65, 69, 77, 80, 83, 84, 87, 89, 97, 101, 104, 108, 110, and all clipart except traffic cone on p. 79; © Visual Mining/Alamy, p. 73.

Cover Illustration: Shutterstock.com (teen girl in car).

Contents

1 Are You Ready? 7

2 Learning the Rules of the Road 17

3 Finally, Rolling 29

4 Licenses 43

5 Cell Phones and Seat Belts: Safety Issues 56

6 Sirens and Lights, Move
to the Right 71

7 Money Matters 88

8 Driving: Environmental Impact 100

Chapter Notes 112

Glossary 122

Further Reading 124

Internet Addresses 125

Index 126

Life is a highway. I want to
ride it all night long.

—Tom Cochrane, "Life Is a Highway"

Are You Ready?

"**W**hen I learn how to drive, I want to get out on the road, get on the highway. I want to drive in the city. I won't have to ask my parents to go to a friend's house. I can do what I want. I can leave the house when I want to. I can go on road trips. I want to go to California."

—D. J., age 15[1]

It was fun to find that shiny quarter under your pillow the first time you lost a tooth. When you turned double digits, you got a birthday bash for all your friends, with pizza, ice cream, cake, and those little paper things that uncurl and make irritating beeps when you blow in them.

Remember the excitement of your very first day at kindergarten and the nervous feeling you had on your first day in high school?

Growing up, you pass a number of milestones, but few of the great events of childhood come close to the thrill of the one you're facing now—learning to drive. The question is, are you ready? Even if you feel that you are ready and you can't wait to get behind the wheel, not everyone is thrilled about this new milestone. You have probably noticed that many people, parents in particular, worry about teens driving. And they have good reason to worry. According to the U.S. Department of Transportation (DOT), car crashes are the leading cause of death for fifteen- to twenty-year-olds. The DOT

believes that the high number of car deaths in young drivers is due to immaturity and lack of experience. Studies show that teen drivers are sometimes over-confident and may take risks that more experienced drivers would not. High-risk behaviors include not wearing seat belts, speeding, and driving while under the influence of drugs or alcohol. The DOT is also concerned about the dangerous habits of using cell phones while driving—text messaging or making phone calls—or using other electronic devices, including DVD players and GPS units.[2]

So, why is there such a difference between teen and adult drivers? Scientists who study the brain have examined some teenagers' risk-taking behavior, and they have learned some interesting things about the teen brain.

Scientists once believed that the brain was fully developed by age twelve. Now, experts have found that this is not true—the teenage brain continues to change. Although the size of the brain stays close to the same, the white and the gray matter continues to grow, bringing with it changes in personality.[3]

The rear part of the brain reaches maturity first. This is the part that controls vision, hearing, touch, and spatial processing. Spatial processing helps you know, for example, that your car will fit into the garage, but not the dog house. This is also the part of the brain that makes it possible to watch out for people on the sidewalk, check your rearview mirror, turn your steering wheel, and use your brakes—all at the same time. They're all essential in being able to safely operate a car.

But the front part of the brain that helps with decision making is the last to mature. This part deals with things like: "What should I do first, text my friend or clean my room?" or "Should I hurry through that yellow light, or should I slow down and stop?"

Fun Fact

In Tennessee, you can't shoot any game other than whales from a moving car.

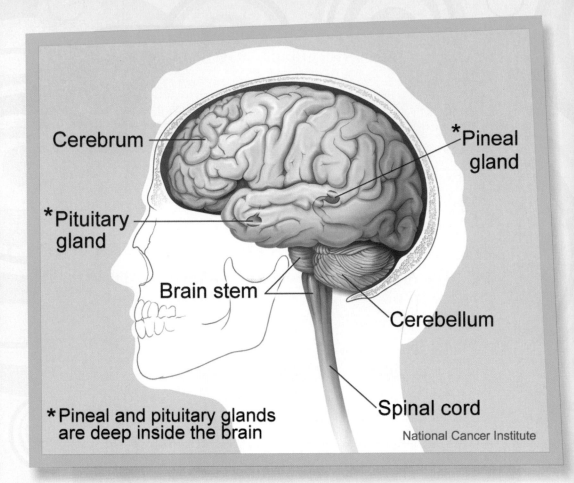

Cerebrum

*Pineal gland

*Pituitary gland

Brain stem

Cerebellum

Spinal cord

*Pineal and pituitary glands are deep inside the brain

National Cancer Institute

New discoveries show that certain parts of the brain mature later than others.

What do these findings about the teen brain mean? Most experts agree that the teenage brain is prone to making risky choices—speeding, texting while driving, or trying to impress their friends by other dangerous, thrill-seeking behavior. A few researchers believe that some teens cannot control their tendency toward risky behavior and that they should not be allowed to drive cars until their brains fully mature.[4]

Getting Ready to Drive

Others believe that teens behave irresponsibly because, in our society, we have low expectations of teenagers. They believe that the brain matures more slowly when we are not required to act maturely.[5]

Even though experts may have different ideas about why the teen brain looks the way it does, most agree that teenagers learn quickly, are intelligent, have quick reflexes, and have superior memory—and that these are all good characteristics to help become safe and responsible drivers.

How Do You Know When You're Ready?

John Miller is a driver education teacher. He believes that nothing you do will come close to being as dangerous as driving a car. Still, it is necessary to learn how to drive, he says, especially if you live in a small town with limited public transportation.

"If you want to get out of here," Miller says. "There is only one way. You have to drive."[6] But Miller believes that we need a better method to determine whether someone is ready to drive. "We have an arbitrary system," he says. "It's called a birth certificate."

Once you reach your state's minimum driving age and pass the written test, you will be allowed to drive on the road. Whether you are ready or not, you will be expected to behave like an adult. "There is a life before driving," Miller says.

"And there is a life after. Before you drive, people cut you some slack, but when you start driving a car, people expect you to be mature."[7]

Karen Sorenson, president of the Wisconsin chapter of Drivers and Traffic Safety Education Association, teaches driver education in the classroom and behind the wheel. She believes that teens who have used riding lawn mowers, or even ridden bikes frequently, are better prepared to head into traffic than those who have not.[8]

"There are, no doubt, numerous valid reasons why a young person may want to learn to drive as soon as possible," says Terry Stark, Motor Vehicle Program Specialist at the Wisconsin DOT.[9] For example, it may be to help with family transportation and getting back and forth to school and work, as well as to extracurricular activities.

Stark believes, however, that not everyone is ready to drive when their birthdays roll around. The decision to begin lessons is an important one that should be given thought and consideration. It is the responsibility not only of the teen but also of parents or guardians, he said.[10]

A study by the DOT emphasizes that parents and guardians need to recognize that getting your driver's license is a very important event. To educate new drivers properly and teach them to avoid high risk behavior, the study says, adults have to look at the role a car can play in a young person's life. "A car represents freedom, excitement, socialization, companionship, and all-around entertainment," the study authors say.[11]

Getting Ready to Drive

Driving can play a pivotal role in a young person's life. It represents freedom and excitement, yet requires responsibility.

What About Learning Disabilities?

If it is difficult to determine brain readiness in your average teen, some teens have an even more difficult time knowing when it is the right time to start learning to drive. Jonathan Jones is on the subcommittee for Learning Disabilities of America. He says that 17 to 20 percent of all teens battle learning disabilities or attention deficit disorders. This may make it both more difficult to learn how to drive and more difficult to recognize the right time to start the learning process.

According to Jones, the most common learning disabilities and disorders that affect teen drivers are visual processing disorders, dyslexia, and attention deficit disorders. These conditions complicate the normal learning process.[12]

Dyslexia is a common learning disability. A person with dyslexia has difficulty processing and understanding written words. The Department of Motor Vehicles will help teens find a way to pass their written exams even if they have difficulties reading. For example, someone may read the exam to a dyslexic person taking the exam.

Jones warns that teens with dyslexia may have problems with ordinary driving tasks, such as reading road signs. They may also have difficulty with less urgent reading tasks, such as reading the car manual or reading directions.

Another common learning disability in teens is visual processing disorder. Unlike teens with dyslexia, those with a visual processing disorder are able to read, but may need more time to make sense of what is happening around them. This may make them slower to recognize or react to hazardous situations, putting them and others at risk.

In addition, attention deficit disorders pose difficulties to safe driving. These disorders' most challenging characteristics are impulsivity and distractibility. Recent studies have shown that youth with attention deficit disorders tend to learn new tasks quicker than other teens. This may mean that those with the disorder may at first be better drivers than other teens. But as soon as driving becomes old hat, Jones says, the impulsivity and distractibility come back. Teens with attention deficit disorders have to take special measures and work extra hard to be safe drivers.[13] Studies show that teens with attention deficit hyperactivity disorder (ADHD) are "two to four times more likely to be injured in a motor vehicle crash than are their peers without ADHD."[14]

But teens with learning disabilities and disorders can still become safe drivers. They just need extra help. The first step is to get the disability diagnosed so the most appropriate help can be found. This is usually something that the school psychologist can help with. The Learning Disabilities Association of America has chapters in all fifty states, and it will help students find the kind of help they need.

Teens with learning disabilities have the same issues to deal with as other teen drivers, only many times worse. Avoiding distractions, such as cell phones and driving with passengers, can help. They should also take precautions to minimize impulsivity, which might lead to speeding and other dangerous risk taking.[15]

Driver education instructor John Miller says that some of his students have special education teachers accompany them to driver education classes. Some students are allowed to take their knowledge tests and their highway signs tests on the computer. Some have the tests read to them.[16]

Are You Ready?

Students with physical handicaps are usually referred to vocational rehabilitation programs, which help people with disabilities. After they receive their learner's permits, they can usually get cars equipped especially for them.

Special consideration is also made for students with language problems. Teens whose first language is not English can usually take the knowledge test in their native language if necessary.

Here We Go

So . . . let's say that you and your parent or guardian have decided that you are ready to learn to drive. This means that you have decided to take on a great adult responsibility. And make no mistake about it, it *is* serious business. Still, with determination and hard work, you can do it!

Learning the Rules of the Road

How to survive America's roads: obey all the traffic laws and assume no one else does.
—Gary Hassler

It's a safe bet that World History, Spanish, and Algebra won't hold your attention quite as well as your driver education class will. After all, you won't get your driver's permit if you flunk this class.

"Some students aren't used to attending classes," driver instructor John Miller says. "One way of failing this class is by not attending."[1]

Understanding traffic signs is important before you ever
venture onto the road.

Getting Ready to Drive

Failing driver education could mean that you have to wait another year for a second chance. In some schools, driver education is only taught every other semester. Also, not all schools and not all states offer driver education in the public school classroom. For some students, private driving schools may be the only option.

But whether you are learning in a public school or in a private driving school, the purpose for the classroom part of driver education is the same. There are certain things you have to learn before you will be allowed on the road, such as traffic signs. Could you imagine the chaos if people who did not know a stop sign from a yield sign, or a merge sign from a no passing sign, were allowed on the highway?

Traffic signs are recognized by shape and color. Though the "stop" and "yield" signs, for example, have words written on them, most signs are made to be understood without words. This helps tourists and other people who do not speak a country's native language get around. Road signs are the same all over the world.

Something else you have to learn in your driver education class is the rules of the road. Every state has its own manual, which is updated annually to list the most recent driving rules for your state. They go by different names in different states— The Motorist's Handbook, Driver Guide, Driver's Handbook, to name a few. But they have one thing in common: you must learn their content before you get your permit to drive.

Learning the Rules of the Road

Here are some things you might learn from your driver's manual, in addition to the road signs:

- How do you get a driver's license?

- What are the Graduated Driver's License (GDL) restrictions?

- What are the seat-belt laws?

- When should you use your headlights?

- When do you need to signal?

- What speed limits are common in what areas?

- How do you merge onto the highway?

- Under what conditions should you not drive?

- How do you parallel park?

- Who gets to go first at an intersection?

- How do you communicate with other drivers?

- What are safe following distances

- What do you do in case of a crash?

Getting Ready to Drive

Driver education is usually an easy class for teens, says Karen Sorenson, classroom driver education instructor. "They *want* to be here. They don't *have* to."[2]

Multitasking—
Not Always a Good Thing

Sorenson tends to trust her students to learn most of the material they need to pass their written tests on their own. She quizzes them in the classroom, and she asks them to review the most important information with each other. But during her lessons, she focuses on things she believes her students may not learn any other way.

One thing Sorenson teaches in the classroom is risk management, which teaches students how to keep dangerous things from happening when they drive. She says:

> I teach the teens that it is not a car, or a truck, or a motorcycle that they see. They need to look *inside* the car, to see that it is a grandmother, or a father, or a child.

> If you look inside the car, you can often see what's going on in there. If the driver is looking down, he or she might be texting. You can also see what is happening with the vehicle. If the front is going down, for example, the driver is braking.[3]

Sorenson tries to help her students learn to read the traffic around them. If you see a car full of people, she says, you might presume that the driver is distracted.

It is now common knowledge that there are a great number of factors involved in a car crash, not just one or two. They may be such things as road conditions, weather, attention, what is happening inside the car, and what is happening in traffic. In Sorenson's driver education classroom, students are asked to read about crashes in the newspaper and to determine which factors contributed to a specific crash.

Sorenson's goal is to empower her students to become safe drivers. She teaches them the importance of wearing seat belts. She tells them to slow down before a stop sign and to pay close attention to traffic around them. She also teaches motorcycle awareness to encourage students to take special care when sharing the road with motorcyclists. And she talks about things to look out for in winter driving, such as potholes and icy roads. And, of course, she tells her students about the dangerous trap of multitasking when driving. While multitasking may be a handy skill in other areas of life, it is never safe to allow anything to distract you while you drive.

For homework, Sorenson's students are asked to learn about the cars they will be driving. They have to find out, for example, where the spare tires and the jacks are located. They have to locate all the inside lights and learn where to insert the gas nozzles to fuel the cars.

22

Getting Ready to Drive

Sorenson also asks her students to interview their parents or guardians. In fact, her students get a list of questions for their parents that they have to guess the answers to *before* they ask. Then they compare their answers with the ones their parents gave them. Some of the questions are: When did you get your license? Did you pass the first time you took your road test? How many times a week will you let me use the car? Who is going to pay for car insurance when I get my license? Who is going to pay for gas? Did you have a curfew when you first got your license? Will I have one? Do I have to change the oil in the car?

To prepare for the written test, Sorenson encourages her students to take practice tests online.[4]

How Do I Get a Permit?

The exact process of getting your permit varies by state. However, most states have similar paperwork requirements. Usually, you have to visit a permit office. This may be the at

Fun Fact

In New York, you may not undress while in your car.

the Department of Motor Vehicles, a police station, or some other state or government office. There you take a written exam, showing that you know your road signs and your state's driving laws.

What to expect from your knowledge test exam varies widely from state to state. Some states make you answer only ten questions, but expect *all* the answers to be correct. Some states allow you to answer only 80 percent of the questions correctly, but they may give you 50 questions to answer. Most states have two parts to their tests: one knowledge part and one part where you have to identify road signs. And some states use hand-written tests, while others allow you to take your test on a computer.

Some Department of Motor Vehicle offices use a computer-based test called QuickFail. The name does not mean that the test is designed to fail you quickly, even though it sounds that way. It means that when you miss a question that takes you over your 20 percent wrong-answer limit, the program shuts down. It is meant to save time and energy. If you fail, you can then go home, study, and come back to take the test again.[5]

Most tests do not have a time limit. But even when they do, most states are generous with their time allotments. If you have studied your material, you should not have a problem finishing on time.

Cheating is not an option, as the person sitting next to you usually has an entirely different set of questions.

PUB 95 (5-09) English Version

pennsylvania
DEPARTMENT OF TRANSPORTATION
Bureau of Driver Licensing
www.dmv.state.pa.us

The first step to getting a permit is studying your state's manual.

Learning the Rules of the Road

After you finish your written exam, you will usually have your vision tested. Different states have different vision requirements, though they tend to be fairly similar.

"We look for 20/40 vision in your best eye," says Patricia Nelson of the Department of Motor Vehicles in Wisconsin. "And your field of vision has to be at least 70 degrees."

If you wear glasses or corrective lenses, Nelson says, you may have a restriction on your license saying that you need to wear them when driving. If you have the restriction on your driver's license and you are not wearing your glasses when driving, it is a citable offense, which means you can get a ticket.[6]

Which documents you need to bring to get a driver's permit also vary. Karen Sorenson tells her students every week what they need to bring to the permit office. But the very last week of their classroom driver education class, students still ask.[7] For specific details of what the requirements in your state are, visit the Web site of your state's department of motor vehicles.

Smile!

Once you have passed your written exam and your vision test, it is time to comb your hair.

Suddenly you find yourself standing in front of a large screen, and your facial expression in the next second will be imprinted on your permit for all your friends to see when they stop by to admire it.

Professional photographer Jean McShane of Northern Portraits says that despite the many bad photos on driver's permits and licenses, there *are* ways to improve your chances of a good picture. When you get up in the morning, McShane says, think about how you dress. Solid colors are better than prints. But most importantly, she says, when you stand in front of the big screen, "Think about something pleasant."

When you think happy thoughts, McShane explains, the muscles in your face relax, which makes for a better picture.[8] Certain licensing facilities will allow you to see your digital image before they print the picture, and you may have an opportunity to retake the photo.

In the end, are you going to want to use this photo for your yearbook? Probably not.

Finally!

Finally, you are ready to wrap it up. In most states, students have to show that they have completed driver education courses before they receive their permits.

Students also have to bring their social security cards, checks for the permit fee (usually very small), and notes from their parents or guardians.

Thinking pleasant thoughts can result in a better photo for your driver's permit.

Since the introduction of the Patriot Act in 2001, student drivers in all fifty states are required to show proof of "authorized presence" in the United States. This means that you must show either that you are a citizen or, if you are an immigrant, that you are in the country legally. For citizens, this proof can be a certified copy of your birth certificate. For immigrants, this may mean showing your green card. Students may also have to show proof that they are enrolled in a behind-the-wheel driver education program. You may be asked for other identification as well, such as a valid passport or a social security card with your signature on it. And, of course, you also have to complete an application.

After jumping over all these hurdles, it is finally in your hand—your permit to drive. And now, you get to turn the key.

Finally, Rolling

Chapter 3

If everything comes your way,
you're in the wrong lane.
—Author unknown

Driving on the interstate was so scary. I'd never gone that fast before. When I hit the reset button for the cruise control, the gas pedal went down by itself. I got distracted and swerved into the oncoming lane. Luckily, it was early in the morning. My teacher was really calm. He didn't even use his brake.

—Hannah, age 15, on her first behind-the-wheel session[1]

On their first day of behind-the-wheel training, students are eager to get rolling. But high school driver education instructor John Miller says, "We always start with the car."[2]

Miller believes it is important that students know their cars well before they start driving. So he teaches them such things as how to open the hood, how to find the radiator, and how to check radiator fluid, oil, and air filters. He encourages them to do the same thing with the cars they will be driving at home. In fact, he tells them to read the entire car manual from cover to cover.

But there is more to learn before they get to push that gas pedal—the inside of the car. "Now we talk about all the gauges," Miller says. "We make sure they can reach all the controls." He points out the windshield wipers, lights, and seat adjustments. "Nobody should have any questions while they're driving," he says. "We need to have that discussion before the car starts moving."

Finally, it is time. Students take their first driving lesson very seriously, Miller says. Sometimes they are nervous. Miller teaches them to relax. If they make a mistake, it will not be the first time that happens, he tells them. "I try to allay their fears while still having them take driving seriously."

Still, it isn't easy to relax when you know that everybody out there has their eyes on you. When you're in the school car, everybody knows you're a beginning driver. "You have a big yellow sign on your head," Miller says.

Getting Ready to Drive

It can be difficult to relax during your first driving lesson. But being familiar with the controls and gauges makes the experience easier.

In addition to learning to relax, the first lesson has a lot to do with keeping your foot on the right pedal. If your foot is not on the brake and your car is in "drive," bad things can happen.

When students have learned to drive in and out of the parking spot, they get to venture out. The first lesson, usually two hours, is spent on quiet streets, making left and right turns, U-turns, driving along a white line, learning the boundaries of the car, and pulling in and out of parking spaces.[3]

Learning to See

Driver education teachers are used to the excitement of riding with a beginner driver. It takes more than a jackrabbit start or a two-wheel squeal around a curve to rattle them. And they do have their own brake if things turn scary.

On the other hand, your parents or other adults driving with you may be nervous the first few times. One of the reasons for their unease is that *they know something you don't!* They know that when the two of you look out the same windshield, you don't see the same thing.

Many studies have been done to understand exactly what a beginning driver sees and how this differs from what an experienced driver sees. Researchers use simulators in which students pretend to drive a car. Students wear high tech glasses that track their eye movements and record where they are looking, or, more importantly, where they are *not* looking.

These studies have revealed some interesting things about new drivers. One study showed that the crash rates of sixteen-year-olds are almost double the crash rates of eighteen-year-olds and almost eight times the crash rates of forty-five- to sixty-four-year-olds, the safest group of drivers.

The study looked at approximately one thousand crashes in which teen drivers were involved. It found that most of the crashes were caused by inexperience. The researchers who did the study believed that the inexperienced drivers did not pay enough attention to what they were doing and that they did not seem to know where to look for dangers. To find out if they were correct in their assumptions, the study authors created a special scene in the simulators. In the scene, a truck was stopped in front of a crosswalk in a suburb. The researchers compared the eye movements of the inexperienced drivers with the eye movements of the experienced drivers as they approached a crosswalk next to the truck (in their simulated cars).

The researchers found a big difference in the way the new drivers and the experienced drivers scanned the scene in front of them. A greater number of experienced drivers scanned both to the left and right of the truck, looking for pedestrians. When passing on the left of the truck, the experienced drivers left room for the unexpected. They slowed down and scanned the area carefully, *again*, before passing the truck. This was not true for newer drivers, who mostly paid attention to what they could actually see.

Fun Fact

In California, it is illegal to use the road as a bed.

What this means is that new drivers need to be aware that they are not yet looking in all the right places and that they need to learn to do so. This is called scanning and using the "what if" strategy.

But fear not. The study also showed that teens who were taught to look for these kinds of dangers very quickly learned to discover unexpected things.[4]

I Love You, You Love Me. We're a Happy Family . . .

"When I was teaching my daughters to drive," John Miller says, "I used to bring other things into the car, like, why is your room such a mess. Those discussions need to be left out of the car."[5]

But it is not only the parents and teachers who need to focus on getting along while driving, Miller says. He is sometimes appalled when he hears how students talk to or about their parents. "That whole disrespect thing," he says. "You can't do that in the car. If you are having a power struggle, you're going to be too emotional and you're not going to see the stop sign."[6] New drivers have to put every bit of their concentration into driving.

Timothy C. Smith, author of *Crash-Proof Your Kids*, recommends a teamwork approach, something worth discussing with your parents before your first lesson.

Having a parent teach you to drive can work with a teamwork approach. It's also important to leave other family issues outside the car.

When teens and parents drive together, Smith says in his book, it is important to find the teen's learning style and to adjust the teaching to it. And here's Smith's twist on the old Dad-teaches-teen-to-drive approach: Smith believes it is a good idea for teens to occasionally get a shot at Dad or Mom, or whoever is the driving teacher. A few examples may be a new teen driver pointing out when a parent rolls through a stop sign, makes an illegal U-turn, or does not follow the speed limit.

This helps teens pay attention to what other drivers do right or wrong. It also evens the playing field and keeps the teacher on his or her toes, making it a lesson for the instructor as well.[7]

Spelling It Out With Mom and Dad—A Parent-Teen Contract

One way of getting along when you drive together is to have things spelled out clearly. Many experts on teen driving, including Timothy C. Smith, suggest using parent-teen contracts. Smith believes in the power of the written word. A written contract may seem formal, he says, but that is the strength behind it. Everybody will benefit from having expectations spelled out, he says.

In the teen part of the contract, Smith discusses such things as commitment to safe, responsible driving; always wearing your seat belt; and ensuring that all your passengers do as well. He talks about promising not to use a cell phone while driving, not exceeding the number of passengers agreed upon, following the speed limit, and not drinking and driving.

The parent or other adult, in his or her part of the contract, has to commit to keeping criticism and yelling to a minimum during driver's training. The adult also promises that if the teen finds himself or herself in a situation where driving is not safe, as in the case of having used alcohol or drugs, the adult will pick the teen up and save the lecture for another time.[8]

Getting Ready to Drive

In summary, a parent-teen contract helps create respect and high expectations of safe driving. It also lets teens know there will be consequences when rules are not followed.

The Road Test

Once you, your driver education teacher, and your parent or guardian feel that you are ready, you may schedule a time to take your road test.

Most state departments of motor vehicles offices will allow you to schedule your road test on the Internet.

Students can get very nervous about taking their road tests. The people who test young drivers tend to take their jobs very seriously, passing only drivers they deem to be safe. They are not likely to chat or joke with you while you take your test. On the bright side, there is nothing mysterious about what you will be asked to do.

Patricia Nelson at the Department of Motor Vehicles in Wisconsin says the road test they have teens perform takes between twelve and twenty minutes. Students need to come prepared to drive in all kinds of road conditions, she warns. They should also have practiced driving in different areas, not just their own neighborhoods. Even though they have passed the written tests, they have to remember their state's handbooks for the driving rules very well. For example, what do you do if an ambulance drives up behind your car with flashing lights while you take your test?[9]

The Crashproof Contract

This agreement reflects our joint expectations, promises and responsibilities with respect to driving and use of a car. We enter this agreement in good faith, having considered these points to be fair, reasonable and in both our best interests.

Teenager

I agree that learning to drive, obtaining my license and operating an automobile are hard-earned privileges, not rights. I will treat these privileges with respect, knowing that demonstrating skill, maturity and good judgment can expand them, and lack of such will lead to restriction or withdrawal of these privileges.

I realize that every time I get behind the wheel I am responsible for my safety and well-being, as well as the safety and well-being of anyone else riding with me. I take this responsibility seriously, and will not knowingly endanger myself or passengers who have entrusted their lives to me.

I will not let anyone else drive a car I am entrusted with, without the explicit consent of both my parents and the other driver's parents.

Seatbelts are mandatory not only for me, but for everyone else who is a passenger in the car. Every time. No exceptions.

I understand that for every passenger in my car I increase the likelihood of a crash by 50%, and I accept full responsibility for the safety of my passengers when I drive. No passengers will ride with me unless I have explicit consent from my parents.

I will not answer or make a cell phone call while I am driving. I agree that no call is so urgent that I can't pull over and make the call when I am off the road.

I agree not to drink any alcohol or take any illegal or mind-altering substances and attempt to drive. I will not get into a car driven by anyone whom I know or suspect has been drinking or taken drugs. If I find myself in this situation I will call my parents for a ride, with no questions asked.

I agree to keep my speed at or below the posted speed limit at all times and to obey all traffic regulations and laws.

I agree to drive with courtesy for everyone else on the road. When other drivers make stupid moves, I understand that it is not about me, and I will not take it personally or show my irritation.

I understand that violation of any of the above may result in the withdrawal, restriction or complete loss of any driving privileges my parents see fit, for a duration they determine.

Parent(s)

I am committed to helping you become the safest, most skilled driver possible, and will spend as much time with you as necessary to accomplish this.

When you are driving I will try my best to limit criticism, shrieking and shouting. I pledge to be patient while you learn.

I acknowledge that I am not a perfect driver, but I have years of accumulated experience and wisdom to share, and no one in the world cares more about you. I will strive to improve my bad driving habits as I try to teach you good ones, and when in doubt, do as I say, not as I do.

If you have been drinking or are otherwise impaired, or if someone driving a car your are a passenger in is impaired and you call me to take you home, I will consider that to be a responsible act, and

I will pick you up without lectures or penalties.

It is my responsibility, and I take it seriously, to reduce, restrict or withdraw any of your driving privileges if I believe it is in your best interest. I don't expect or need you to agree with or like those decisions. I don't like to make them, either. It's totally up to you to avoid them.

It will also be my pleasure to grant, expand or accelerate your driving privileges as you earn them, and I will be proud to do so.

_____   _____

Teen's Signature   date

_____   _____

Parent(s) Signature   date

Teen driving expert Timothy C. Smith provides his students with copies of this contract for teen drivers and their parents to go over together.

Road test examiners take their jobs seriously because they are responsible for deciding whether someone is ready for a driver's license.

Before the road test, the examiner conducts an inspection of the car. It is a good idea to carefully check your car before you come in. "We cannot conduct the test if the car is not up to code. This includes having a valid registration," says Nelson.[10]

Nelson has seen many sad sixteen-year-olds who could not take their tests because of cracked windshields, burned-out turning signals, or invalid vehicle registrations.

When the vehicle inspection is done, it is time to sit down behind the wheel. The examiner, Nelson says, will not usually be chatty and conversational. He wants the person taking the test to focus on driving. The examiner never asks the driver to do anything illegal. He never tries to trick you by telling you to do something he will take points off for. Instead, he will give clear instructions, telling you to, for example, turn right the first time it would be legal to do so.

One of the things examiners look for is how well the driver checks his or her blind spots. "You should check your mirror, then signal, then look over your shoulder," Nelson says. "You should also check blind spots whenever you pull away from a curb and when you make lane changes."[11]

Not checking your blind spots may cause you to fail your road test. Another reason someone might fail is not coming to a full stop at a stop sign. Speeding is another big one. Students sometimes have the idea that they're allowed to speed "a little," Nelson says. That's not true. Even driving one mile per hour over the speed limit might cause you to flunk the road test.

Not everyone passes their road tests the first time around. If it happens to you, don't be discouraged! It means you have more time to really get it down.

After the road test, examiners take the driver to a "station" for feedback. Here, examiners tell you if you passed or not. If you did not pass, you will be told exactly why so you can go home and practice in order to pass the next time.

Getting Ready to Drive

Licenses

> **E**verything in life is somewhere else, and you get there in a car.
> —E. B. White, *One Man's Meat*
> (Tillbury House Publishers, 1943)

It seems obvious that in order to operate an almost three thousand pound chunk of metal that can reach speeds of 150 miles per hour or more, one should need some sort of proof that one knows how to handle this beast. Let's say, um, a license of some kind.

It was not always like this. In fact, people in the United States drove for many years without any kind of proof that they knew how to do it. But as cars became more popular and more people were driving them without any training, car accidents became more common as well. Some people were upset about all the crashes and car-related deaths. The public demanded some sort of test.

The United States wasn't the first country to have its people pass tests before being allowed to drive. At the turn of the twentieth century, France and Germany had started requiring people to get driver's licenses before operating motor vehicles on public roads. On August 1, 1910, New York became the first U.S. state to require a driver's license, though, at first, it was only required for professional drivers. In 1913, New Jersey became the first state to require a license of *all* drivers, not just professionals.

What Now?

So after months of studying, taking behind-the-wheel lessons, and practicing with your parents, you finally took your road test . . . and passed! You finally have your driver's license in hand. Now what?

The second time she took her road test, sixteen-year-old Emma passed with flying colors.

"Oh my God, you have no idea how good it felt to pass," Emma says. "Last night I was so nervous, I almost started to cry. I was shaking. I couldn't sleep. I wanted it so bad. Now my parents don't have to drive me everywhere. I feel so free."[1]

Getting Ready to Drive

A Little Piece of Plastic

Emma and other teen drivers who pass their road tests will be given what in many states is called "a probationary license with GDL [graduated driver licensing] restrictions." These restrictions are different in every state.

Before the year 2000, it would have been almost impossible to write about driver licensing in a way that was true to all states. Licenses were too different, and the states all had their own

Finally getting that little piece of plastic is a cause for celebration for many teens.

ideas about how they should look. After 2000, however, states started working together on the Driver's License Agreement. The goal was to make licenses more similar, which would help law enforcement be more efficient in, for example, accessing people's records.[2]

Today, the color, format, and security features of your license are made to be easily recognizable across state lines. The font is usually large so it can be read quickly. The color and the writing all have different meanings. Not all states are using these color codes and the shapes yet, but eventually, driver's licenses across the nation will look very similar, maybe even identical.

The license itself is usually pink, to look different from state-issued identification cards. The words *Driver's License* are color coded on most cards. Black means occupational license; this is a temporary license for people who have had their regular licenses revoked or suspended. An occupational license may be used, for example, when driving to and from work. Green is a commercial license for people who drive large buses or trucks. Blue is a regular license. Red is a probationary license.[3]

These color codes were created so that police officers could quickly recognize what kind of license someone has. Teen drivers' licenses are particularly easy to identify this way. When you are under the age of twenty-one, your license is often vertical instead of horizontal. To make it even clearer, white print on red background means you are under twenty-one. Black print on yellow background means you are under eighteen.

The color codes and the shapes also make it easier for an officer to see whether a driver has GDL restrictions on his or her license. And it makes it easier for someone who works in a bar to determine whether a patron is under the legal drinking age.

The Gift of Life

So now you have it: your very own piece of plastic with your very own picture smiling back at you. Having solved the mystery of the color coding, there may still be things you wonder about, such as the anatomical gift statement.

You may have seen a bumper sticker reading: *"Don't take your organs to heaven. Heaven knows we need them here."* Perhaps the thought of your body being in a condition where people would take your organs makes you shudder. As a teenager, you probably have not considered what you would like to happen to your body when you die. But when you die, someone might be able to use your organs to help save the life of someone who is critically ill. On the back of your new driver's license, you will find something usually called an "Anatomical Gift Statement." That is another way to say "organ donation." Now is as good a time as any to make up your mind about being an organ donor.

It is not an accident that Trey Schwab is the outreach coordinator for the University of Wisconsin Health Organ Procurement Organization. He is a good choice for that position because he is an organ recipient himself.

Schwab knows what it means to be given a second chance at life. A few years ago, when he worked as the assistant coach for the Marquette University basketball team, he was diagnosed with an incurable lung disease. His doctors told him that if he did not receive a transplant, he would die within three years. Schwab was lucky. After waiting two years, he received two new lungs and a second lease on life. Many people are not so lucky. According to Schwab, nearly one hundred thousand people across the country are waiting for new organs. Each day, eighteen people die because they do not receive help in time.

"We all have a number of organs that can be donated," Schwab says. "Heart, lungs, liver, kidneys, pancreas, and intestine. Then there are corneas and numerous other bone, skin, and tissue items that can help up to 100 other people."[4]

It is not pleasant to think about a crash horrible enough that we no longer need our kidneys, or our corneas, or our skin. Still, choosing to donate your organs on your license may help in unexpected ways. If something *does* happen to you, your loved ones may be comforted knowing that your organs are helping someone else stay alive. And perhaps, thinking about our own mortality can teach us to drive more carefully.

The organ donation check box on the back of your driver's license is not a legally binding contract, however. If you are a minor, your parents or guardians will decide what to do with your body if you die in a crash. But checking the anatomical gift statement box is an important way to make your wishes known to your loved ones.[5]

This bumper sticker urges people to donate organs. You can indicate on your driver's license whether you wish to be an organ donor.

Graduated Driver Licensing

Chances are that when your parents or guardians got their licenses, it was a low-key affair. They may have learned to drive in driver education classes, then taken their tests, easily passed, and voilá, they had their licenses. Right away, they could drive carloads of friends to the local skating rink, with no restrictions whatsoever. Not so anymore. If you have worked hard and practiced many hours, you may pass the driver skill test. But this does not mean you get to load your car up with friends for a trip to the beach. You get a license, but it comes with important restrictions.

Some of the restrictions on your license have to do with wearing glasses or corrective lenses, or, if you have a physical handicap, perhaps with needing adaptive equipment in the car. These restrictions may also be found on the back of an adult's driver's license. But if you are a teenager, there are

restrictions that only have to do with age and inexperience. These often determine when you can have other teen passengers in the car, the hours that you can drive, and the use of cell phones.

Teens are sometimes irritated by these restrictions. It is convenient to be able to pick up your friends on the way to school in the morning, not to mention bringing them home after a late soccer practice. But when you take a closer look, these restrictions may make more sense.

Many Words, Same Thing

Whether you call it a graduated driver's license, GDL, or probationary license—and whatever you think of it—there are some convincing statistics that a restricted license is a good idea. A 2006 study published in *Pediatrics* shows, on average, graduated driver licensing decreases fatal crashes among sixteen-year-olds by 11 percent. This number is based on the less restrictive GDL. The states with the strictest GDL requirements reduced their teen crash rates even more, up to 21 percent. This means that restrictions are proven to save more than one in five teens from dying in a car crash.[6]

The idea behind the GDL is to require three stages of learning to drive, which will give you more driving experience while under some supervision:

Getting Ready to Drive

(1) First you get your learner's permit. During this period you have an adult in the car with you, at all times, when you drive. This stage ends when you pass your road test.

(2) Next comes an intermediate stage in which you have limited unsupervised driving in high-risk, meaning real-life, situations. You drive without another driver, but have restrictions regarding who can be in the car when you drive and what time of day you are allowed to drive.

(3) Finally, if all goes well, you receive your regular driver's license. At this point, all restrictions are lifted.[7]

Studies have found that the most effective GDL requirements have to do with implementing age requirements and passenger restrictions, limiting night driving, having a three-month or longer waiting period from the time you get your learner's permit until the time you are allowed to test for your license, and requiring thirty hours or more of supervised driving.[8]

Not all states use meaningful GDL laws, though all states have some sort of restrictions on new drivers. Most states, however, are noticing lower death rates among teens following GDL restrictions. As of February 2010:

- Thirty-three states have a minimum requirement of thirty supervised driving hours, ten or more of which are performed at night with limited visibility. Many of these states require fifty supervised driving hours.

- Forty-nine states and the District of Columbia have nighttime driving restrictions during the second stage of the GDL.

- Forty-three states and the District of Columbia have restrictions on the number of teen passengers allowed during the second stage of the GDL. A number of states allow *no* underage passengers in the car during the second stage of driving. California, the strictest state in this regard, allows no passengers under the age of twenty for the first twelve months of driving, unless the driver is supervised by someone age twenty-five or older.[9]

Although these restrictions may seem inconvenient, it is probably a safe bet to assume that the restrictions will be even more stringent in the years to come. The more we learn about safety and teen driving, the more we recognize how vital the GDL has been in better traffic safety.

Most GDLs have a limit on the number of underage passengers in a car.

Monitoring Devices

As soon as you start driving alone, your parents or guardians may have another trump card up their sleeve—parental monitoring devices. Through the use of cameras, GPS devices, and microphones in the car, parents can learn about their teen's driving activities, even when the teen is driving without them. The devices can answer such questions as: Are they speeding? Where are they? How are they driving? These devices are becoming more popular, and like the GDL, they save lives.

American Family Insurance offers its clients a parental monitoring device it believes will help keep teens safe while lowering insurance costs. Together with a company named DriveCam, it created Teen Safe Driver. Here is how the program works. A small camera is placed behind the rearview mirror of the teen-driven car. Whenever an "event" occurs in the car—the driver brakes suddenly, swerves, or in other ways acts erratic—the camera saves a few seconds worth of tape before the event as well as a few seconds after.

DriveCam receives the recorded information, transferred wirelessly to its analysis center. It analyzes the footage and then tries to determine what happened. Its interpretation of the event is shared with the driver and the driver's parents or guardians so the driver can correct the behavior that led to "the event" that set off the camera.[10]

In 2006, a nine-month study of fifty-four families in Minnesota and Wisconsin showed a more than 70 percent reduction in "high-risk driving events" among participants enrolled in the Teen Safe Driver project. Seat-belt use improved from 50 percent to almost 100 percent among teens in the study. The most surprising result was that the teens liked participating in the study. They believed that the program helped them become better drivers.[11]

Getting Ready to Drive

Not everyone is enamored of these new devices. One *New York Times* writer calls the technology "Electronic Leashes for Teenagers" and likens them to an extension of the nanny cam, a way for employers to monitor their nannies without the nannies' knowledge. Shouldn't teenagers be given the chance to solve their own problems in preparation for life in the adult world?

"Every teenager must eventually wander into the wrong neighborhood," he writes, "and then, without parental assistance, figure out how to wander back out."[12]

According to American Family Insurance, the risk of a crash increases 700 percent when a teen is no longer driving with a parent or a guardian. In light of such overwhelming statistics, perhaps it is worth putting up with a little inconvenience for the first twelve months of driving.[13]

Cell Phones and Seat Belts: Safety Issues

Chapter 5

> **I**t doesn't matter how high you scored on your SAT if your head is smashed against the windshield. You must be alive if you're going to follow your dream.
>
> —Driver education teacher John Miller

It is impossible to discuss driving safety in a meaningful way without mentioning the frightening statistics.

Did you know that sixteen-year-olds are three times more likely to die in a car crash than other drivers? And that is just *one* scary fact. Here's more:

- In two-thirds of the crashes in which teens are killed, inexperience is the main reason for the crash.

- More than two-thirds of teens killed in car crashes are not wearing seat belts. If there are two or more teen passengers in the car (with a teen driver), the crash risk is *five* times as high as when there is just one or no passengers.

- Two-thirds of all teens who die in car crashes are passengers of teen drivers.[1]

Funeral director Marcus Nelson does not embalm "statistics" or spend hours and hours stitching up faceless numbers. He deals with real people, with names, and with families who love them. When someone dies in a car crash, Nelson is often the person called to the scene to bring the body home.

"At the funeral home, I have to put the person back together," Nelson says. "If the last time the family saw him, he was getting in a car, healthy and normal, it's hard for them to get through the grief process. It helps to see the body."[2]

Nelson spends a lot of time working on making the dead look peaceful for the family in order for them to feel closure. When it comes to car crashes, he has seen more than he cares to talk about.

"I've seen things twisted in directions in which they shouldn't be twisted," he says. "Legs that are mangled to barely hanging on, or gone altogether. I've seen someone hit the

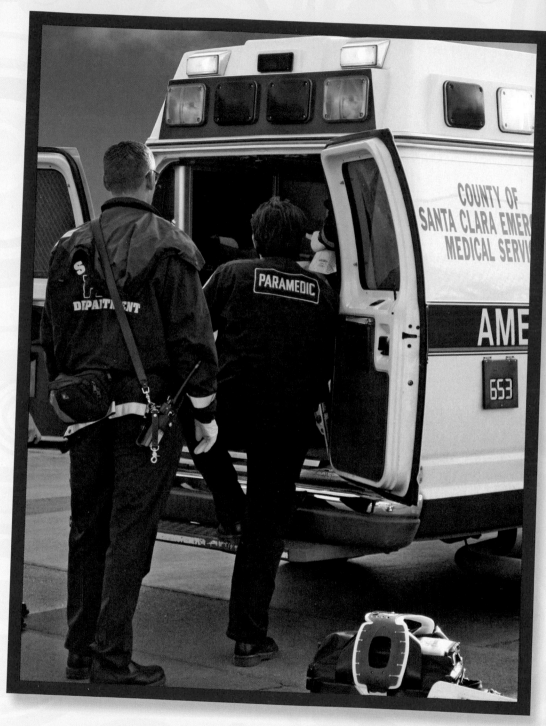

Statistics on vehicle crashes and young drivers are sobering and scary.

steering wheel with such force that they had a steer
pattern imprinted on their chest. Some people break
and the ribs puncture their hearts and lungs. It's r
instant. It could be a matter of minutes before they die.

It is so emotionally difficult to pull someone's broken body from a car wreck that Nelson focuses on the small details, such as, how do I get this leg unstuck? Sometimes he notices disturbing signs in the car, such as a cell phone on the floor or scattered food remains.

The natural thing for people to do when they hear of a car crash, Nelson says, is to distance themselves. The first thing we think about is how the crash has nothing to do with us. "But sometimes it *is* us," Nelson says. "Or someone we know. It's not always about someone else."[3]

Experience Is Key

"If we're hunting, most of us want to go with an experienced woodsman," John Miller, driver education instructor, says. "That person knows how to look for signs. An inexperienced driver doesn't know how to look for signs or how to adjust their driving behavior."[4]

"Driving safely requires practice," says Terry Stark at the Department of Transportation.[5] It might sound like an obvious statement, but some studies show that most teens are not worried about their lack of experience. Newly licensed, many feel that they are already great drivers.

In a study of young male teen drivers, the teens were asked to rate their driving skills. On a scale of one to ten, with ten being the highest score possible, most of the teens gave themselves an eight. More than half the males in the study group had been involved in a car crash *before* they answered the question.[6]

"Teens believe they are invincible," driver education teacher Karen Sorenson says. "If you ask them if they are a good driver, they will all say they are."[7]

"The one thing that unites all human beings, regardless of age, gender, religion, economic status or ethnic background, is that, deep down inside, we all believe that we are above average drivers."
—Dave Barry, "Things That It Took Me 50 Years to Learn," *Dave Barry Turns 50* (New York: Ballantine Books, 1999), p. 181

Although some experienced drivers also fall into these traps, common mistakes typical of beginners include following too closely behind another car, speeding, getting easily distracted, focusing only on the car in front of you while ignoring signs of danger elsewhere, and not wearing a seat belt.

Following too closely. In one study, teens said they disliked when people tailgated them. They found it "dangerous and annoying." However, they all said they tailgated people they thought drove too slowly. They believed they could "react in time if the car in front stopped suddenly."[8]

Getting Ready to Drive

It is dangerous to assume that you can stop in time, says an American Automobile Association study. Tailgating is a leading cause of deadly car crashes among teens.

There is, however, an easy way to prevent tailgating crashes—the famous three-second rule. It is estimated that it takes a minimum of three seconds from the time you see a hazard on the road ahead until your brain tells you about it and your foot finds the pedal and stops the car. This means that if you make sure you have a "three-second" distance between you and the vehicle ahead, you will be a safer driver.

Leave sooner, drive slower, live longer.

—Author unknown

Many young drivers tailgate. Inexperience makes it hard for them to estimate safe following distances and stopping times.

Cell Phones and Seat Belts: Safety Issues

It is easy to estimate the distance between yourself and the car in front of you. When the car ahead of you passes a stationary object, such as a light post, begin counting: "one thousand one, one thousand two, one thousand three." Not before you reach the last word, "three," should your car pass the same object.

In case of bad weather, the distance needs to be greater than three seconds.

Speeding. Speeding is not just a problem among male drivers (or teens, for that matter), but because the study above discusses these issues, we will look at the example of the male teens again.

The teen drivers in the study felt that driving five to ten miles above the speed limit was necessary to keep up with traffic. Those who routinely sped reported that they felt confident that they could handle the car just as well at the higher speed.[9]

One study sponsored by the Children's Hospital of Philadelphia indicated that 38 percent, or more than one third, of fatal crashes by male teen drivers involved excessive speed. In an article, "Top 10 Mistakes Young Drivers Make," author Kelsey Mays says that though many people speed occasionally, teens speed "because they don't have a good sense of how a car's speed can affect their response time."

Speeding might, in fact, be a part of teen risk-taking behavior due to the developmental stages of the teen brain, Mays says. When studying two different areas of the brain, "one that triggers impulsive actions and one that reins them in," researchers found twice as much activity in the part of the brain that triggers the impulse. The two areas of the brain did not have equal amounts of activity until the person turned twenty years old.

Another problem when discussing speeding is defining exactly what it means. Speeding is not just driving faster than the speed limit allows. At times, to be safe, you must, in fact, drive *slower* than what is allowed. So you are not only speeding when you drive 60 mph in a 55 mph zone but also when you travel too fast for the road conditions—for example, taking a curve too fast on an icy, wet, or sandy road.[10]

"It takes 8,460 bolts to assemble an automobile, and one nut to scatter it all over the road."

—Author unknown

Distractions—cell phones. Watching the scenery, talking on the cell phone, adjusting the radio, checking your GPS, texting, talking to other passengers, swatting at a bee, eating— these are activities people sometimes engage in while driving, And they are all activities that take the driver's attention away from the road—if only for a few seconds.

If you drive 55 miles per hour, you move about 80 feet per second. If you react quickly, you might be able to start breaking in two seconds. This means that before you even *begin* putting the pedal down, you have traveled 160 feet, almost half a football field.

Now imagine that you are looking into your lap for two short seconds, so you don't even notice the hazard popping up in front of you. Half a football field has zoomed by before you realize there is danger!

Distracted driving among teen drivers becomes even more dangerous when cell phones are involved. A recent study by the Children's Hospital of Philadelphia and State Farm Insurance showed that only one quarter of teens believed that cell-phone use while driving put them at a higher crash risk. In comparison, more than three quarters of the teens asked believed that texting while driving was dangerous.

Although teens did not think talking on the phone in itself was a hazard, most believed it was dangerous when the phone call triggered emotions. Eighty-nine percent of the teens reported "often" seeing other teens using cell phones while driving, and 71 percent said they had seen the driver upset and emotional because of the phone call.[11]

There are currently not many statistics that show how dangerous it is to use a cell phone while driving. Many teens do not live to answer the question about what caused their crashes, and many who do survive do not admit to talking on the phone or texting while driving.

Unfortunately, hands-free devices do not appear to be any safer. A study published in January 2010 by the Highway Loss Data Institute concluded that there had been no reduction in accidents in states where bans on using hand-held phones while driving were instituted and where people were still allowed to talk on hands-free devices. Talking on the phone while driving, whether on a hand-held phone or a hands-free device, appears to be a very dangerous activity.[12]

Distractions—other passengers. The more friends in the car, the merrier, right? Wrong! There is no good news when it comes to friends in the car. Every teenager you add to a car greatly increases your risk of a crash. With one passenger, the risk increases 40 percent. With two, it doubles, and with three or more, the risk for a crash is almost four times that of driving alone.[13]

Using a cell phone while driving—for either talking or texting—is highly dangerous.

Focusing only on the car in front of you. "Teens have not yet developed the ability to 'scan' far ahead and to the sides, as they drive," says a Children's Hospital of Philadelphia report. "They also don't detect hazards, such as pedestrians or roadside objects, as quickly as adults."[14] As we learned from the study that looked at eye movements of an experienced driver and an inexperienced driver as they approached a computer-simulated crosswalk, teens have yet to learn where to look. However, that study also showed that with good training, teens could learn this vital task quickly.

Lack of seat-belt use. Two-thirds of teenagers killed in car crashes in 2005 were not wearing their seat belts. A Department of Transportation study from that year shows that teens are less likely to wear seat belts than persons of any other age group.[15] They are also much more likely to be in a car crash.

Fun Fact

In North Carolina, it is illegal to drive on sidewalks.

Getting Ready to Drive

Researchers are puzzled by teens' lack of seat-belt use. Some studies found that seat-belt use could lower your risk of dying in a car crash by 50 percent.[16] Most teens seem to have heard these statistics, but according to the study above, many have a puzzling attitude when it comes to wearing seat belts. About half the teens asked thought that in the event of a crash, belts were "as likely to harm as to help," and others felt that "a crash close to home was usually not as serious." Teens quoted in the study did not want to wear their belts when their friends didn't. They also said the belt made them "worry more about being in an accident."[17]

In another study, teens said they did not want to wear belts because they were only traveling a short distance, that their clothes got wrinkled, and that it wasn't cool.[18]

A Wisconsin study found that 57 percent of teens in car crashes wore their seat belts when alone in the car. When they drove with friends, only 49 percent wore belts. The same study found that 54 percent of female crash victims wore seat belts, but only 38 percent of male victims wore them.

There are two different kinds of safety-belt laws. One is called a primary law, the other, a secondary law. In states with primary seat-belt laws, an officer can stop you and ticket you for noticing that you are not wearing a belt in the car. In states that have a secondary seat-belt law, you may only be ticketed for not wearing your seat belt if you are stopped for *another* infraction and the officer notices that you or your passengers are not wearing belts.

Of all the ways to be safer on the road, the statistically most important—and the easiest—is this: buckle up.

Fatigue. It seems most teens understand the risks of texting while driving, and most definitely know the dangers of driving drunk or under the influence of drugs. What seems to be more of a gray area, some researchers found, is fatigue. In several studies, teens reported driving while fatigued or seeing other teens drive fatigued. According to the Children's Hospital of Philadelphia, the effects of driving while tired are similar to those of driving under the influence of alcohol. Drivers under age twenty-five are the cause for most car crashes where fatigue is a major factor.[19]

July and August—danger on the road. A study done by the American Automobile Association (AAA) foundation in 2006 drew the conclusion that July and August are the deadliest months for teenagers when it comes to car crashes. During these months, teens had more free time to drive around with their friends. Teens from states with stricter GDL laws had fewer crashes than teens from states with less-strict laws or less enforcement of the laws.

The time of the day and the day of the week were also factors in teen crashes, according to a 2007 Wisconsin Division of Motor Vehicles study. The time of day with the most teen car crashes was between 3 P.M. and 4 P.M.—shortly after school gets out. The most dangerous day, regardless of the season, was Friday. In addition, for the northern states, December and January were found to be dangerous months because of ice

Getting Ready to Drive

Fatigue makes drivers less alert and slows down reaction times.

and snow on the road.[20] Interestingly, a study by the Children's Hospital of Philadelphia showed that children who rode with a teen driver who was a sibling were 40 percent *less* likely to be in a crash than those who rode with teens they were not related to.[21]

Not wearing a seat belt and deliberately speeding put teens at risk more than any other age group. This is both bad news and good news—bad news because teens get injured and die unnecessarily, and good news because it means you have control over your behavior and can choose wisely.

There is other good news as well, buried in these scary statistics. In a study called "Teen Unsafe Driving Behavior," researchers learned something that most teens already know—although teens respond poorly to preachy messages about, for example, seat belts and speeding, they do respond well to *facts*. Teens in the study were willing to listen to *real* facts about safety and driving statistics and to change their driving habits when they had learned *why* their driving behavior was unsafe.

With more factual information about driving safety issues, teens can make better choices about their driving habits.[22]

Sirens and Lights, Move to the Right

Chapter 6

> **T**he best car safety device is a rearview mirror with a cop in it.
>
> —Dudley Moore

We have been told how dangerous it is for teens to drive, so why then are there so many crashes that have nothing to do with teens? The truth is, it *is* more dangerous to drive when you have a brand-new license, but age and experience do not make you immune from having a crash. There are many car crashes among people of all age groups. There are even certain risk factors that are more common in older drivers, such as drinking and driving. Some teens do drink and drive, but usually, drinking and driving is a greater problem among older age groups, since teens are not allowed to drink alcohol. And aggressive driving and road rage are problems that affect more experienced drivers as often as teen drivers. These are just a few examples of driving-related risk factors that are not teen-specific. Here again, there are many things you can do to stay safe. And when a crash does happen, there are a number of things you can do to protect yourself from further damage.

Drinking and Driving

We learn to drive before we can legally drink alcohol. So drinking and driving should not be a problem for teens. Right?

Though drinking is not one of the leading causes in crashes for teens, it is still a concern. And after the first few years of driving, when it becomes legal to drink, the number of crashes that involve alcohol rises sharply. Another thing to think about when it comes to drinking and driving is that even if you are sober, not everybody else on the road is. Drunk drivers share the road with you. Even if you do everything you can to avoid a crash, drunk drivers are still a danger.

The state with the worst drinking and driving record is Wisconsin. Fifteen percent of adult drivers said they had driven under the influence of alcohol in the past year. State officials believe the real number is even greater, closer to 25 percent.[1]

Adults driving drunk are a big problem, but, as mentioned earlier, teens are not entirely innocent when it comes to drinking and driving. In one study, teens said they believed that drinking and driving was one of the most unsafe things teens did. But several of them also said they had driven after drinking. They gave three reasons for drinking and driving: 1) Because they were underage, they were

A temporary memorial at the site of a fatal crash. Drinking and driving are a deadly combination.

Sirens and Lights, Move to the Right

afraid to call their parents; 2) they had to get home and had no other way to get there; 3) they weren't thinking.[2]

What's so bad about drinking and driving anyway?

You would be able to tell if you couldn't drive safely, couldn't you? Not necessarily. According to the New York State Department of Motor Vehicles, *any* amount of alcohol affects your ability to drive safely. When you drink, it becomes more difficult to judge distance and speed—two things that are important when you drive. Young drivers lose this ability even more quickly than older drivers, after drinking only very small amounts of alcohol. Coffee, cold showers, and walks will not sober you up more quickly. Time is the only thing that will make you sober after drinking.[3]

Alcohol is not the only thing that slows your reflexes. Not surprisingly, drugs have a huge impact on driving ability. A study by the National Highway Traffic Safety Administration and Maastricht University in the Netherlands found that the use of marijuana slowed drivers' reactions by 0.9 seconds when they were moving at a speed of 59 miles per hour. Thus, subjects traveled an additional 78 feet before they could stop. The *combination* of marijuana and alcohol, the study said, slowed a person's reactions by 16 seconds or 139 feet—almost double.[4] It should also be noted that alcohol and drugs affect each individual differently. Depending on a person's weight and metabolism, he or she may be affected differently by the same amount of alcohol.

Getting Ready to Drive

So although drugs and alcohol may make some people feel more confident—and even make them believe they are better drivers—these substances are proven to be dangerous, even deadly, in combination with driving. As with many other risk factors when it comes to driving, there is a solution: don't drink or use drugs and drive.

Road Rage and Aggressive Driving

According to National Highway Traffic Safety Administration, aggressive driving occurs when "an individual commits a combination of moving traffic offenses so as to endanger other persons or property."[5] Or, in plain English, aggressive driving is when someone gets angry while he or she drives and then does something stupid or dangerous.

For three years in a row, Miami, Florida, has held the title of worst city for road rage in the nation, according to the news agency Reuters. Researchers believe this may have to do with the mix of cultures present in Miami, as well as the fact that Florida attracts many retired people who drive slowly, sightseeing while young professionals are in a hurry to get places.

In a telephone survey, more than 2,500 persons were asked what made them angry when driving. What seemed to annoy people the most was when others texted or talked on cell phones while driving. Other factors inciting road rage were seeing people speeding, tailgating, running a red light, or changing lanes without signaling.[6]

YIELD

Aggressive driving is often the cause of road rage. In a study of aggressive drivers on the Capital Beltway around Washington, D.C., researchers learned that aggressive drivers got angrier than other drivers when cut off or when someone drove faster than they did. They often honked, cursed, and tried to cut the other driver off.[7]

Teen drivers are not immune to road rage or aggressive driving. If anything, teens may battle quickly changing emotions even more than adult drivers. In a study by the Children's Hospital of Philadelphia, it was determined that teen drivers with heightened emotions, positive *or* negative, were more prone to road rage. More than half the teens in the study had seen other teen drivers display road rage when driving.[8]

Moreso than driving while fatigued, talking on cell phones, having multiple passengers in the car, or not wearing a seat belt, driving with strong emotions was viewed by the Children's Hospital of Philadelphia as driving under "extremely dangerous conditions."[9]

What to Do When You Get Stopped

No matter how careful you are, at some point you may see lights in your rearview mirror, flashing just for you. Even if you did not speed, the officer in the patrol car behind you may have cause to pull you over. Your headlights might be out, you might have been swerving, or you might not have been wearing

Road rage can be a reaction to aggressive or inattentive drivers.

your seat belt, which can get you pulled over in some states. Whatever the reason, do not worry. Most officers will be nice and polite, especially if you behave respectfully. Hopefully, you have learned this little rhyme in your driver education class: *Sirens and light—move to the right.*

Don't panic when you see the twirling lights, State Trooper Tim Smith advises. "Stay calm, and gradually pull over to the right side of the road as soon as it is safe."[10] Many of the people Smith stops immediately start rooting around for their driver's licenses and their insurance information. It's a no-no, Smith says.

"When you open a console and reach for something, we may think you're reaching for a weapon. We prefer that you leave your hands on the steering wheel."

As the officer approaches your car, you should roll down the window, smoothly, without sudden movements, Smith advises. Then return your hands to the steering wheel.

"Keep your hands where we can see them," he said.

The hand advice goes for other passengers as well. It is an important precaution for state troopers' safety. Tell your passengers to stay calm and to show their hands. And whatever you do, do not get out of the car, Smith warns. Many state troopers have been injured in traffic when they approached a stopped car, so they have now started approaching cars on the passenger's side instead of the driver's side. This is sometimes alarming to people who are not aware of the policy change.

Smith emphasizes the need for mutual respect when you are stopped on the highway. The first thing he does is introduce himself. Then he tells the driver why he was stopped.

"I will give the driver respect, and that is all I ask in return," Smith says. "You may not agree with this citation or this ticket, but there is a system in place. Take it to the system. Don't argue with an officer."

Smith will ask to see the driver's license. In some states, the driver will also have to present the vehicle registration and proof of insurance. Then Smith asks about the reason for the stop. He might say, for example, "Did you see the red light back there?" He is specific about what will happen next. For instance, he might state, "You will receive a citation for speeding today."

Then Smith returns to the patrol car to process paperwork. When he comes back to the car, he gives the driver the ticket. State Trooper Smith often finds out after he stops a teen driver that he or she was preoccupied with talking on the cell phone or texting and did not notice that he or she was speeding.

If you are stopped by a police officer, remain calm, stay in the car, and keep your hands on the steering wheel.

"Texting is a huge problem," he says. "It's a major distraction. I have seen many crashes where kids have been texting. When you're driving, that's what you're supposed to be doing, just driving the car. Cell-phone use can be very dangerous."

When Smith checks a teen's driver's license, he looks for GDL requirements.

"We enforce the GDL rules 100 percent," he says. "This could mean that one of your two friends will have to find another ride home, something that might be difficult and embarrassing."[11]

Getting Ready to Drive

1. When you see the lights flashing in your rearview mirror . . .

Do pull over to the right and stop.

Don't keep driving on the right side of the highway.

2. When an officer approaches your vehicle . . .

Do stay in your seat with your hands on the steering wheel and remain in your car.

Don't start looking for your license and your insurance information.

Don't get out of the car—unless requested to do so by the officer.

3. When the officer tells you why he or she stopped you . . .

Do talk politely and show the officer the documents he or she requests.

Don't argue and tell the officer that you didn't do it.

Sirens and Lights, Move to the Right

Another result of getting stopped with a GDL violation is that you may get double points for violations. Your driver's license might be suspended, in which case you have to wait longer for your permanent license.

Steer It and Clear It—What to Do When You Are in a Crash

Driving statistics are frightening. And yes, they are even scarier for teen drivers than for more experienced drivers. There is no way to make driving look less dangerous than it is. Statistically, it is likely that you will be in a car crash at some point. If you are, and if you are not seriously injured, there are ways in which you can make things easier and keep the costs down.

In many states, there are laws about moving your vehicle after a crash. These laws go by different names, such as "Move It" or "Steer It, Clear It." These laws tell you to move your vehicle to the side of the road if it can be moved and if nobody is hurt. This is so people will not get hit while waiting for emergency vehicles.[12]

Some people worry that if the vehicle is moved, it will be more difficult for insurance agents and police to figure out what caused the crash, but State Trooper Tim Smith says this is not usually the case. Since the law was passed more than ten years ago, police and insurance agents have not had more difficulty in determining the cause of the crash. The bottom line is, this law helps make people safer in traffic.[13]

Dial 911 in an Emergency

If you or someone else is injured, and you are able to, says Smith, you should call 911 immediately. "Don't move injured people, unless you are medically trained. And unless the car is on fire, wait for the EMTs to arrive."[14] Make sure you are in a safe place where you are not in danger from traffic. Be prepared to tell the operator where you are, your cell-phone number, and what the problem is. While you wait for help, try to get information about the others involved in the crash: write down their names, addresses, insurance companies, car makes and models, license plate numbers, and driver's license numbers.[15]

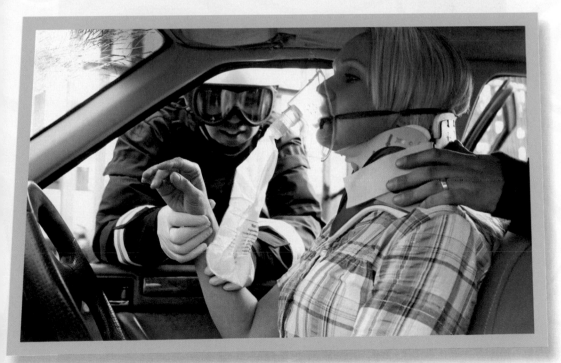

Rescue workers help an injured woman. If someone is hurt in a crash, call 911 and wait for the EMTs.

Sirens and Lights, Move to the Right

Police officers can use radar guns to detect your speed. Some teens who have practiced on a race track seem to forget that they're on a regular road and go way beyond the speed limit!

In rural areas, hitting wild animals, especially deer, is common. If you hit and kill a deer, report the crash to the local sheriff's office or police station. In many states, when you hit and kill a wild animal, you may keep the animal, but it has to be tagged.[16]

Never leave the scene of a crash when someone is hurt or when you have damaged something that doesn't belong to you without reporting it. That is called a hit and run, and it is illegal.

Performance Training

What if I don't want to be an inexperienced driver? Couldn't I just go to a racetrack and train—learn to *really* drive?

There are different thoughts about "motorsports performance training." Some people think it is a good idea to learn how to take corners quicker or to drive at high speeds. The Children's Hospital of Philadelphia does not believe this is safe, however. Statistics show that teens who have taken performance training have higher crash rates. Training gives teen drivers a false sense of security, and they may actually speed and drive more recklessly.[17]

The bottom line when it comes to driving safety, says John Miller, driver education instructor, is to keep learning every day of your life. Whether you just got your license or you are an experienced forty-five-year-old driver, you will have to make decisions about safe choices every day.

"Computer games have a reset button," Miller said, "but if you roll your car and have permanent nerve damage, you don't get to rewind and start over."[18] If you engage in reckless behavior on the road, you will have to live with the consequences for the rest of your life.

Brakes

A discussion about driving safety would not be complete without mention of . . . brakes!

Before you even start your car the very first time, you need to find out whether the car has regular brakes or ABS brakes.

ABS stands for Anti-Lock Braking System. Almost all new cars have them. There is also a difference between four-wheel and two-wheel ABS. Four-wheel ABS brakes will allow you to better steer around obstacles while braking.

ABS brakes, which do not need to be "pumped" like older brake systems, will not allow you to stop more quickly, as some people believe, but they *will* prevent skidding. Although ABS brakes and regular brakes work almost the same during normal conditions, the kind of brakes you have will change the way you handle emergency situations. Also, while ABS shortens the braking distances on firm surfaces, it has been known to lengthen the distance on loose gravel or dirt. This is one of the reasons why it is important that you know your brakes and how they work.

Another advantage to driving a car with ABS brakes is that most car-insurance companies will give you a discount for having them.

Money Matters

> **C**ar sickness is the feeling you get when the monthly payment is due.
>
> —Author unknown

Most teen drivers can come up with many good reasons why they should have their own cars, the most powerful one being transportation. Having your own car will make getting to and from school and after-school activities a lot easier. Not to mention getting to and from work. What can you do to get your own car? In most states, if you are under the age of eighteen, you are not allowed to sign a financing agreement unless you have someone co-sign.

When shopping for a car, either new or used, it's a good idea to visit a reputable dealer.

So when you go car shopping, bring Mom, Dad, or someone else authorized to act as your financial sponsor.

Most teens looking for a car do not have a great amount of money and will have to settle for buying a used car.

"They have to buy what they *can* buy," says Joe Turner, owner of Turner Chevrolet-Cadillac in Park Hills, Missouri. He emphasizes the importance of buying something you can afford. When we buy a car, he explains, our eyes are often bigger than our pocketbooks. "Make sure you match your car with your budget," he says.[1] Keep in mind not only the initial cost of the car itself but also the maintenance costs and the insurance rates.

Using a reliable car dealer is a good plan, Turner says. If you live in the same town as the car dealership you are using, you may know the dealer's reputation. Unlike a private seller you found over the Internet or via an ad in the local paper, a dealer will be there for you if you have questions or concerns later on.

The very best used cars, Turner says, are usually traded in to the dealers toward new cars. These used cars become available for sale at the dealership. Reliable car dealers count on people coming back in the future. They want to make their customers happy so they return to buy their next cars.[2]

So what should you look for when buying a new car? A good place to start is to look at what you *shouldn't* buy. Some studies show that sporty cars with high performance features are not great for teen drivers. Teens are more likely to drive dangerously and take risks when driving such vehicles. Teens also have a bad history of roll-overs in sports utility vehicles, more so than older drivers. And, because of money issues, teens often end up driving cars that are older and less safe than those of more experienced drivers.[3]

Even with money restrictions, there are things you can do to get the best possible vehicle within your budget. First of all, you want to make sure you do not end up with a car with mechanical problems, Turner advises. Ask the person you are buying the car from whether you can take the car to a mechanic and have it checked out.

Getting Ready to Drive

Turner also advises young customers to consider how much they are willing to pay in car insurance before they settle on a particular car. A high performance car will come with higher insurance rates, he says. You also want to consider such things as how much will you be driving; what kind of gas mileage do you expect, or can you afford; can you afford the upkeep of this particular car? And consider the state tax, which will add to the price of the vehicle.[4]

The American Automobile Association (AAA) lists a number of considerations for buying a car. It suggest you check the odometer reading to see how many miles the vehicle has traveled. It tells you to also ask for a maintenance record of the vehicle. If this is not available, find the service facility that worked on the car in the past in order to get more information. Signs that a car has been repainted might indicate that it has been in a crash. Other things to check thoroughly before you buy are brakes, badly worn tires, water damage, windows, doors, locks, and automatic seat adjustments. AAA also advises prospective buyers to listen to the engine for odd noises and to make sure that all the lights work as they should.

Once you have done the stationary check, AAA suggests that you take the car for a test drive to look for the following things:

The steering wheel should not be wobbly or difficult to turn.

The automatic transmission and acceleration should be smooth, without strange knocking sounds.

A car salesman hands over the keys to a customer. Teenagers usually need a parent or guardian with them when buying a car.

Brakes should work smoothly, and you should be able to stop the car suddenly.

There are also commercial businesses that, for a fee, can help you learn more about the history of your car. Some car dealers even offer this kind of service for free. Be sure to ask.

Although he understands the budget limitations of teens buying a car, Joe Turner warns, "The cheapest car won't be the best one. It's cheap for a reason."

Sometimes it is better to pay a little more up front and have lower costs later. Paying more for a car might mean better fuel economy and lower cost for repairs and insurance.

Car Maintenance

You may have a new car, or a used one; you may drive your own car or one belonging to your parents. Whatever the case, taking good care of the car you drive is an important part of your new life as a driver.

In addition to the obvious task of keeping the car clean and rust free, the most important way to increase the longevity of your car, according to auto mechanic Jon Johnson, is regularly changing your oil. Some people believe you can go longer between changes with newer cars, but Johnson recommends that you change your oil every 3,000 miles or, if you do not drive long distances, every three to six months. Leaving your oil in too long, Johnson says, will create oil deposits that restrict flow. This puts the engine at risk. Air and oil filters and all fluid levels should also be checked and changed regularly.[5]

In a study by State Farm Insurance and the Children's Hospital of Philadelphia, researchers learned that only one-fourth of teens were required by their families to take financial responsibility for vehicle repairs or maintenance. Thirty-nine percent of students surveyed said they were not asked to be responsible for *any* car-related expenses. Most commonly, teens were asked to cover some of the fuel costs.

YIELD Auto Insurance

"Insurance is the promise that if something happens to you while you drive your car, someone else will accept responsibility," says State Farm Insurance Agent Tim Reedy.[6] He often talks to students in driver education classes about the importance of insurance. Buying insurance is not like buying a sweatshirt from your local store. "It's not an object you can touch with your hands," says Reedy.

To show how insurance works, Reedy passes around an empty jar to the students. Then he collects imaginary insurance fees. One person is told to put in a hundred dollars, another, to put in fifty. Yet another student has to put in three hundred. When Reedy asks the students what strikes them about this system, the first answer he usually gets is, "It's not fair." Reedy agrees. Insurance is not a fair system. Or rather, he says, "It is both fair and unfair. Every single person that comes into my office and asks for an insurance quote will get a different answer."

There is a reason why everybody is treated differently. Understanding this reason may make the system seem a bit less unfair. Reedy says the reason some people pay more and some people pay less for the same insurance coverage is, "statistics, statistics, statistics!"[7]

Here are a few things, according to Reedy, that help decide how much you will pay:

Age—The younger you are, the more you pay. Why? Younger people statistically have more crashes than more experienced drivers.

Gender—Whether you are a boy or a girl affects how much you pay. Why? "Statistically speaking, young males are in more crashes than young females," Reedy says. According to many insurance companies, a female driver is considered a "youthful operator" until the age of twenty-five. A male driver is considered a "youthful operator" until the age of thirty—unless he is married. Because married drivers are statistically less likely to have crashes than unmarried drivers, married men are considered "youthful" until the age of twenty-five.

Grades—Why grades? Students with a grade point average of 3.0 or above are statistically less likely to have a crash than those with lower grades. There could be a number of reasons for this, but perhaps the most obvious one is that students with higher grades tend to be more responsible, making sure their homework, reports, and projects are done on time. These students may also be more conscientious drivers, staying under the speed limit and following safety rules, which makes them less likely to have crashes.

How you will use your vehicle—The more you drive, the higher the cost. Though, the more you drive, the faster you gain experience, it is also true that the more you drive, the more likely you are to be in a crash.

The kind of vehicle you drive—A sports car is more expensive to insure than a sedan, for example. The cost of the vehicle and the cost of repairs are an important factor.

Your driving record—Yup, getting a ticket will affect your insurance rates. More tickets means higher insurance rates.

Your history with the company—If your family uses the same company for other insurance, such as home, health, or life insurance, you may pay less for your car insurance.

Your family's credit history—"Your family credit history is a better indicator than anything else as to who will have a crash," says Reedy.[8] Again, this has to do with responsible behavior. This does not mean that if your family has a poor credit history, you are doomed to have a crash—statistics are only numbers—but in this instance it does mean that you will have to pay more for your insurance.

Number of cars in your household—Another thing that helps decide how much you will pay for insurance is how many cars your family has per driver.

If you are the "principal" driver of a car (if you have your own car), you will pay much more for car insurance than if you are a "secondary" driver (you drive someone else's car). The insurance company looks at how many drivers you have in your family, and how many vehicles. If there are more drivers than vehicles, you will probably be considered a secondary driver,

Getting Ready to Drive

Colorful Cars

Despite their reputations, red cars do not cost more to insure than cars of other colors. However, insurance for sports cars is more expensive.

Everybody knows that a red car costs more to insure than a blue car. Right? Wrong! Reedy gets the car color question all the time when he visits driver education classes. But what is true is that sports cars are more expensive to insure, and sports cars are often red. Drivers of sports cars are more likely to be involved in crashes, and the vehicles are expensive to repair.[9]

Very little research has been done regarding car crashes and car color. According to research from the American Automobile Association from 2004, there is nothing that indicates that a car of one particular color would be more likely to be involved in a crash than a car of a different color. What researchers do know, however, is that red, which is the color of fire engines and many other emergency vehicles, is one of the most difficult colors to see. For better visibility, optometrists suggest using lime yellow on emergency vehicles.

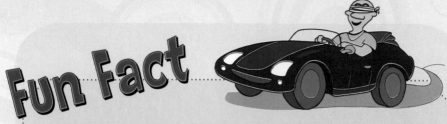

which means you will have lower rates. If there are more cars than drivers (or the same number), you will be considered a principal driver, which means higher rates.

To protect those who might get injured in an auto crash, all states require by law that drivers carry liability insurance. In Wisconsin and New Hampshire, drivers have to show financial responsibility if they do not wish to purchase insurance, which means they have to show proof that they are able to pay for damages if they injure someone in a crash.

Bodily injury liability is the part of your insurance that pays the medical bills for the people you might injure who are not your passengers. Property damage liability covers damages caused to someone else's property, such as a car or a mailbox.

You might also consider collision insurance, which will pay for the repairs on your car if you collide with something. Comprehensive insurance covers what the insurance companies call "acts of God and vandalism," such as hitting an animal that jumps out in front of you, a rock flying onto your windshield and cracking it, or a tree falling on your car.

Personal injury protection (PIP) pays for medical bills for you and your passengers if you are injured in a crash.

The last of the more common coverage to consider when buying car insurance is uninsured or underinsured motorist's coverage. This is the insurance that helps pay your bills if someone who runs into you is not covered by insurance and is unable to pay your bills.[10]

"Driving a brand-new car feels like driving around in an open billfold with the dollars flapping by your ears as they fly out the window."

—Gray Livingston

Helping With Payments

Driving is expensive. It is important to know all the costs involved before you run out and buy your own car. Even if you drive your parents' or your guardian's car, you probably have to pay for some things, such as the added cost of insurance, gasoline, regular upkeep, or repair of the car.

Remember, before you start driving, you are allowed to make mistakes, but after you get your license, you are expected to act like an adult. This is certainly true in regard to the way you handle your money. Not being able to pay for a movie ticket is a minor problem compared to running out of gas on the highway and not having enough money to fill the tank so you can get home. When you start driving, not only do you have to be emotionally mature in order to avoid crashes, you also have to be financially mature so you can pay for the added cost of driving.

Driving: Environmental Impact

Chapter 8

> Modern technology
> Owes ecology
> **An apology**
>
> —Alan M. Eddison

We've all heard it, maybe even more often than we care to: cars pollute the environment and contribute to global climate change. You might think, "It's not going to make a difference if I drive my little car to the store instead of taking a walk or riding my bike." But, it *does* make a difference. One fourth of the energy consumed in the

Burning gasoline pollutes the air and contributes to global climate change.

world goes to transportation.[1] That's us, you and me, driving to the soccer field, or to the grocery store, or to school.

Burning fuel produces biproducts, such as carbon dioxide. When you drive your car, fuel is burned, and carbon dioxide is released into the atmosphere. Carbon dioxide traps heat in the atmosphere and contributes to global climate change.[2]

There are other byproducts of burning fuel as well, including nitrogen dioxide, sulphur dioxide, benzene, formaldehyde, and polycyclic hydrocarbons. These gasses can make it difficult for people to breathe, especially in areas with dense population and lots of traffic.

But environmental reasons aren't the only arguments for keeping driving to a minimum says Environmental Studies professor Dorothy Lagerroos. There are political reasons as well. The United States consumes an incredible amount of oil every year. Because the United States does not produce enough oil on its own, it relies on foreign countries. This reliance can sometimes cause political conflict.

Cars also encourage inefficient use of land. Houses and stores are built far away from each other because cars make it easy to move from place to place. If we had to walk or bike to the store, we would live closer to it and leave more land in its natural state.

But there are alternatives, Lagerroos says. You do not have to drive everywhere you go. In urban areas, you may take a bus or a commuter train to reach almost any part of the city. Even in rural areas, it is sometimes possible to walk or bike.[3]

Getting Ready to Drive

So What Can I Do?

The driver handbook for many states encourages new drivers to consider alternatives to driving. The Wisconsin Motorist Handbook, for example, tells new drivers that by planning ahead, they can save fuel and time. Use public transportation whenever possible, it says. Avoid driving during rush hour because stopping and starting frequently is a fuel guzzler. Call ahead and make sure that the store has that item you need, and combine errands to avoid unnecessary driving.[4]

Hypermilers and Eco-drivers

Then there are the *serious* fuel savers. Hypermiling is becoming a better-known activity among some drivers. It basically means driving more energy efficiently than the Environmental Protection Agency (EPA) estimates that your car can drive. For example, if you have a car that is advertised as driving 45 miles per gallon, a hypermiler might be able to drive 60 miles per gallon with that same car.

Peter Valdes-Dapena, a staff writer for CNNMoney.com, has a number of money- and energy-saving tips for drivers. He advocates using your cruise control on the highway. Speeding up and slowing down uses a lot of fuel. Setting your cruise control helps you stay at the same speed. He also advises against slamming your brakes or making sudden and quick starts. Basically, the more smoothly you drive, the more gasoline you save.

Using your cruise control on the highway saves fuel. Although you may have to do less in terms of pedal work while in cruise control, you still have to stay alert and pay attention to the road.

Calculating Fuel Use

Here's an easy way to learn how much gasoline your car uses.

- Write down your car's mileage or reset your trip meter to zero.
- Fill up your gas tank all the way.
- Drive the car until you need to fill it up again.
- Fill up your gas tank all the way.
- Deduct the old mileage from the new mileage to find out how many miles you drove since you last filled up. Or, if you reset your trip meter, note the current mileage.
- Check to see how many gallons of gasoline you purchased.
- Divide the number of miles by the gallons of gasoline and you will know how many miles per gallon (mpg) you got out of your last tank of gas.

Hypermilers go even further. Wayne Gerdes of Wisconsin holds the Hybridfest record for driving the most fuel efficiently. Hybridfest is an annual event in Madison, Wisconsin, where hybrid car drivers get together and celebrate their fuel-efficient vehicles.

Gerdes actually invented the term "hypermiling." Gerdes wants to help lessen the U.S. dependency on the Middle East for oil. He started paying attention to how, by driving his car differently, he could save a great amount of gas.

By watching his fuel-consumption display (a feature in some new car models that shows your current miles per gallon use), Gerdes knows the speed at which his car is most fuel efficient. He tries to drive at this speed as much as possible.

Hypermilers call their fuel consumption display their "game gauge." They treat hypermiling like you might a computer game, always trying to find ways to beat their old record.

Gerdes and other hypermilers move their foot off the gas pedal long before they arrive at a red light. They try to time their arrival so it involves as little braking and as little acceleration as possible. Gerdes takes everything that is not needed out of his car. Extra weight adds mileage. He drives with his windows up and the air-conditioning off. His tires are filled to the specification of his car's manual, and he never carries a rack on the roof. Keeping your tires properly inflated is good advice for all drivers because it can give you a whopping 6 percent improved fuel efficiency.

Getting Ready to Drive

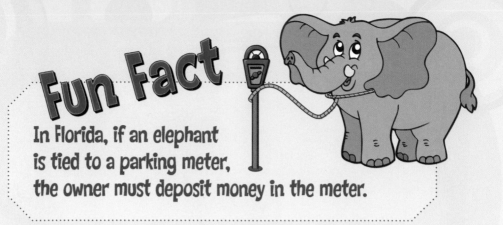

Fun Fact

In Florida, if an elephant is tied to a parking meter, the owner must deposit money in the meter.

In Europe, classes that teach "ecodriving," which "supports energy efficient use of vehicles," are becoming more popular. In Sweden, you can no longer pass your driver's test unless you pass the ecodriving part. Both the written and the behind-the-wheel tests have ecodriving components. At Axelsson's Driving School in Västerås, Sweden, they have taught ecodriving for more than ten years. It is all about common sense, they say. You lift your foot off the gas pedal as soon as you see a red light. Ecodriving, the Swedish instructors say, can lower your fuel consumption by 10 to 20 percent. Swedish ecodriver teachers travel all over the world to teach this commonsense driving method.[5] You may not be ready to throw out the passenger seat to get rid of extra weight or risk suffering heat stroke by keeping your windows up and the AC off. But there are many things we can learn from the hypermilers and from Swedish ecodrivers, such as using your pedals gently. This will not only help save money and lessen the carbon footprint on our planet, but less-aggressive driving is also safer driving.

Take your car to a mechanic for regular tune-ups. A well-maintained car helps save fuel.

By all means, try to get the best possible mileage out of your car, but play it safe. Safety should always be your top priority when you are behind the wheel. Fuel economy can come second.

Hypermiling is just one way to save money and to reduce pollution. Another way to help save the environment, though not necessarily your wallet, is to drive a hybrid car. A hybrid car gets its name because it uses at least two different power sources, most commonly an electric and a gasoline-fueled engine. Although not all hybrid cars get excellent gas mileage, they do, as a rule, pollute less than other vehicles.

According to auto mechanic Jon Johnson, another way to keep from polluting is changing your oil, as well as your air and fuel filters, regularly.[6]

Driving in an environmentally friendly manner is yet another way in which you can establish that you are a mature, responsible driver.

If, when reading this book, you were confronted with dire statistics and a worrisome prognosis about your driving future, do not despair. Driving is a serious activity that requires maturity. But you can make smart choices that will make you a better, safer driver. Being a safe, responsible driver comes with great rewards, such as the continued freedom of sharing the roads with other drivers.

"Every time I see an adult on a bicycle, I no longer despair for the future of the human race."

—H. G. Wells

If you ride your bike instead of drive whenever possible, you are playing a small but significant part in reducing pollution.

Discussion Questions

1) Do you believe that teens are babied in society today? Why or why not? Do you believe that how people treat you could actually make your brain develop differently? And do you think that the way the teen brain works affects the way teens drive?

2) How much do you believe your parents will let you use the car once you have your license? Do you think they will expect you to pay for gas? What about repairs? Will you have to change the oil? Do you think they will make you pay for the increased insurance cost?

3) If you were to write a parent-teen contract, what would be in it?

4) Which of the GDL requirements make good sense to you? Which ones would you get rid of if it were up to you? Why? Why do you think these were put in place? Do you think the time frames in your state are appropriate?

Chapter Notes

Chapter 1: Are You Ready?

1. Personal interview with D. J., April 23, 2008.

2. "Teen Unsafe Driving Behaviors," *National Highway Safety Administration,* September 2006, <http://www.nhtsa.gov/people/injury/newdriver/teenunsafedriving/images/TeenUnsafeDriving.pdf> (April 4, 2011).

3. Claudia Wallis, "What Makes Teens Tick," *Time,* September 26, 2008, <http://www.time.com/time/magazine/article/0,9171,994126,00.html> (June 16, 2011).

4. Ibid.

5. Robert Epstein, "The Myth of the Teen Brain," *Scientific American,* vol. 17, no. 2, June 2007, pp. 68–75, <http://www.scientificamerican.com/article.cfm?id=the-myth-of-the-teen-brain> (April 4, 2011).

6. Personal interview with John Miller, April 9, 2008.

7. Ibid.

8. Personal interview with Karen Sorenson, April 9, 2008.

9. Phone and e-mail interviews with Terry Stark, March 10 and March 20, 2008.

10. Ibid.

11. "Teen Unsafe Driving Behaviors," p. 44.

12. Telephone interview with Jonathan Jones, May 21, 2008.

13. Ibid.

14. Committee on Injury, Violence, and Poison Prevention, and Committee on Adolescence, "The Teen Driver," *Pediatrics*, vol. 118, no. 6, December 2006, pp. 2570–2580.

15. Telephone interview with Jonathan Jones, May 21, 2008.

16. Personal interview with John Miller, April 9, 2008.

Chapter 2: Learning the Rules of the Road

1. Personal interview with John Miller, April 9, 2008.

2. Personal interview with Karen Sorenson, June 13, 2008.

3. Ibid.

4. Ibid.

5. Personal interview with Patricia Nelson, June 12, 2008.

6. Ibid.

7. Personal interview with Karen Sorenson, June 13, 2008.

8. Personal interview with Jean McShane, July 22, 2008.

Chapter 3: Finally, Rolling

1. Personal interview with Hanna, July 29, 2008.

2. Personal interview with John Miller, April 9, 2008.

3. Ibid.

4. Alexander Pollatsek, Vinod Narayanaan, Anuj Pradhan, and Donald L. Fisher, "Using Eye Movements to Evaluate a PC-Based Risk Awareness and Perception Training Program on a Driving Simulator," *Human Factors*, vol. 48, no. 3, Fall 2006, pp. 447–464.

5. Personal interview with John Miller, April 9, 2008.

6. Ibid.

7. Timothy C. Smith, *Crash-Proof Your Kids: Make Your Teen a Safer, Smarter Driver* (New York: Fireside, 2006), pp. 31–35.

8. Ibid., pp. 238–239, 243–245.

9. Personal interview with Patricia Nelson, June 12, 2008.

10. Ibid.

11. Ibid.

Chapter 4: Licenses

1. Personal interview with Emma, July 10, 2008.

2. Brian Bergstein, "National Uniform Driver's License Law Is 'Nightmare,'" *USA Today*, January 12, 2006, <http://www.usatoday.com/tech/news/techpolicy/2006-01-12-uniform-drivers-license_x.htm> (April 4, 2011).

3. "Wisconsin's Driver License/Identification Card," *Wisconsin Department of Transportation*, July 3, 2008, <http://www.dot.wisconsin.gov/drivers/drivers/apply/types/digital.htm> (August 4, 2010).

4. E-mail interview with Trey Schwab, May 11, 2008.

Getting Ready to Drive

5. Personal interview with Patricia Nelson, June 12, 2008.

6. Susan P. Baker, LiHui Chen, and Guohua Li, "Graduated Driver Licensing Programs and Fatal Crashes of 16-Year-Old Drivers: A National Evaluation," *Pediatrics*, July 2006, pp. 59–60, <http://pediatrics.aappublications.org/cgi/content/abstract/118/1/56> (April 4, 2011).

7. "Graduated Driver's Licensing (GDL) Laws," *Governors Highway Safety Association*, April 2011, <http://www.ghsa.org/html/stateinfo/laws/license_laws.html> (April 4, 2011).

8. Baker, Chen, and Li, p. 56.

9. "Graduated Driver's Licensing (GDL) Laws."

10. American Family Insurance, *Teen Safe Driver Program*, n.d., <http://teensafedriver.com> (July 23, 2008).

11. Ibid.

12. Joe Queenan, "Good Fences; Electronic Leashes for Teenagers," *New York Times*, May 24, 2001, <http://query.nytimes.com/gst/fullpage.html?res=9907E4D7133DF937A15756C0A9679C8B63> (April 4, 2011).

13. American Family Insurance.

Chapter 5: Cell Phones and Seat Belts: Safety Issues

1. "Share the Drive: The Whole Truth About Teen Driving. 10 Things People Don't Know About Teen Driving," *The Children's Hospital of Philadelphia*, August 2007, <http://www.teendriversource.org/tools/support_teens/detail/31> (April 4, 2011).

2. Personal interview with Marcus Nelson, April 29, 2008.

3. Ibid.

4. Personal interview with John Miller, April 9, 2008.

5. E-mail interview with Terry Stark, March 20, 2008.

6. "Teen Unsafe Driving Behaviors," *National Highway Safety Administration,* September 2006, p. 34, <http://www.nhtsa.gov/people/injury/newdriver/teenunsafedriving/images/TeenUnsafeDriving.pdf> (April 4, 2011).

7. Personal interview with Karen Sorenson, June 13, 2008.

8. "Teen Unsafe Driving Behaviors," p. 18.

9. Ibid., p. 14.

10. "TheParent/Teen Driving Agreement," *The Children's Hospital of Philadelphia*, May 9, 2008, <http://www.teendriversource.org/more_pages/page/the_parentteen_driving_agreement/for_parents> (March 11, 2008).

11. Flaura Koplin Winston, Dennis R. Durbin, Suzanne D. Hill, Lauren P. Hutchens, and Tracey A. Hewitt, "Driving: Through the Eyes of Teens," *The Children's Hospital of Philadelphia,* 2007, p. 11, <http://stokes .chop.edu/programs/injury/files/PCPS_ Reports/1289teen.pdf> (April 4, 2011).

12. "Laws Banning Cellphone Use While Driving Fail to Reduce Crashes, New Insurance Data Indicate," *The Highway Loss Data Institute*, January 29, 2010, <http://www.iihs.org/news/rss/pr012910.html> (August 4, 2010).

13. Committee on Injury, Violence, and Poison Prevention, and Committee on Adolescence, "The Teen Driver," *Pediatrics*, vol. 118, no. 6, December 2006, pp. 2570–2580.

14. "Keeping Young Drivers Safe."

15. "Increasing Teen Safety Belt Use: A Program and Literature Review," *Department of Transportation*, September 2005, DOT HS 809 899, <http://www .nhtsa.dot.gov> (May 9, 2008).

16. Ibid.

17. Ibid.

18. Committee on Injury, Violence, and Poison Prevention.

19. "Share the Drive."

20 Laura C. Andréason, "Wisconsin Crash Facts on the 16- to 19-Year-Old Age Group," *Wisconsin Department of Transportation*, October 2008, <http://www.dot.wisconsin.gov/drivers/teens/ docs/teenfacts08.pdf> (April 4, 2011).

21. "While Caution Is Warranted, Child Passengers Are Safer When Teen Driver Is Their Sibling," *The Children's Hospital of Philadelphia*, June 14, 2007, <http://www2.prnewswire.com/cgi-bin/micro_ stories.pl?ACCT=159681&TICK=CHOP&STORY=/ www/story/06-14-2007/0004608252&EDATE=J un+14,+2007> (June 11, 2008).

22. Teen Unsafe Driving Behavior," p. 20.

Chapter 6: Sirens and Lights, Move to the Right

1. Kevin Freking, "Study: Midwest Has the Worst Drunken Driving Rates," *Washington Post*, April, 4, 2008, <http://www.washingtonpost.com/wp-dyn/ content/article/2007/08/22/AR2007082201987 .html> (April 4, 2008).

2. "Teen Unsafe Driving Behaviors," *National Highway Safety Administration,* September 2006, p. 39, <http://www.nhtsa.gov/people/injury/newdriver/ teenunsafedriving/images/TeenUnsafeDriving.pdf> (April 4, 2011).

3. "You and the Drinking Driving Laws," *New York State Department of Motor Vehicles,* March 2008, <http://nydmv.state.ny.us/broch/C-39DDL-web .pdf> (July 24, 2008).

4. Kelsey Mays, "Top 10 Mistakes Young Drivers Make," *Cars.com,* June 1, 2007, <http://www.cars .com/go/advice/Story.jsp?section=yd&subject=yd_ shop&story=ydTop10&referer=advice&aff=cartalk> (April 4, 2011).

5. "Aggressive Driving," *National Highway Traffic Safety Administration,* n.d., <http://www.nhtsa.dot.gov/Aggressive> (May 9, 2008).

6. Irene Kuan, "Miami Voted Worst City for Road Rage: Survey," *Reuters,* May 13, 2008, <http://www.reuters.com/article/2008/05/13/us-driving-roadrage-idUSN1350920020080513> (May 14, 2008).

7. "Aggressive Drivers," *National Highway Traffic Safety Administration,* n.d., <http://www.nhtsa.dot.gov/people/injury/enforce/aggdrv.html> (May 9, 2008).

8. Flaura Koplin Winston, Dennis R. Durbin, Suzanne D. Hill, Lauren P. Hutchens, and Tracey A. Hewitt, "Driving: Through the Eyes of Teens," *The Children's Hospital of Philadelphia,* 2007, p. 15, <http://stokes.chop.edu/programs/injury/files/PCPS_Reports/1289teen.pdf> (April 4, 2011).

9. "What's Killing Our Teens? U.S. Survey Describes the Factors Contributing to Vehicle Crashes," *State Farm Insurance,* January 25, 2007, <http://www.statefarm.com/about/part_spos/community/sflocal/california/20070125.asp> (April 4, 2011).

10. Personal interview with Tim Smith, May 13, 2008.

11. Ibid.

12. "Quick Clearance," *Federal Highway Administration,* n.d., <http://ops.fhwa.dot.gov/eto_tim_pse/about/qc.htm> (July 24, 2008).

13. Personal interview with Tim Smith, May 13, 2008.

14. Ibid.

15. Ibid.

16. "What to Do If You Hit a Deer," *Motorists'
    Handbook, Wisconsin Department of Transportation,*
    May 2010, p. 58, <http://www.dot.state.wi.us/
    drivers/docs/e-handbook.pdf> (April 4, 2011).

17. "Keeping Young Drivers Safe: Performance
    Training," *The Children's Hospital of Philadelphia,*
    March 11, 2008, <http://www.chop.edu>
    (May 9, 2008).

18. Personal interview with John Miller, April 9, 2008.

Chapter 7: Money Matters

1. Telephone interview with Joe Turner, April 13,
   2008.

2. Ibid.

3. Committee on Injury, Violence, and Poison
   Prevention, and Committee on Adolescence, "The
   Teen Driver," *Pediatrics,* vol. 118, no. 6, December
   2006, pp. 2570–2580.

4. Telephone interview with Joe Turner, April 13,
   2008.

5. Personal interview with Jon Johnson, June 5,
   2008.

6. Personal interview with Tim Reedy, May 29, 2008.

7. Ibid.

8. Ibid.

9. Ibid.

10. Ibid.

Chapter 8: Driving: Environmental Impact

1. Stefan Theil, Akiko Kashiwagi, Quindlen Krovatin, and Stepher Glain, "7 Ways to Save the World," *Newsweek (Atlantic Edition),* vol. 149, January 29, 2007, pp. 40–45, <http://www.newsweek.com/ 2007/01/28/davos-special-report-7-ways-to-save- the-world.html> (April 4, 2011).

2. Personal interview with Dorothy Lagerroos, May 23, 2008.

3. Ibid.

4. "Before You Drive, Plan Ahead . . . Save Fuel," *Motorists' Handbook, Wisconsin Department of Transportation,* May 2010, p. 7, <http://www.dot .state.wi.us/drivers/docs/e-handbook.pdf> (April 4, 2011).

5. Alison Hawkes, "Sweden Requires Fuel-Efficient Driving Lessons," *National Public Radio,* August 8, 2008, <http://www.npr.org/templates/story/story .php?storyid=93408952> (April 4, 2011).

6. Personal interview with Jon Johnson, June 5, 2008.

Glossary

ABS (antilock braking system)—A type of brake that prevents skidding.

aggressive driving—Driving that occurs when someone commits a combination of moving traffic offenses so as to endanger other persons or property.

anatomical gift statement—A statement on the driver's license regarding organ donation in the event of the driver's death.

bodily injury liability—The part of insurance that pays the medical bills for the people you might injure who are not your passengers.

collision insurance—That which pays for car repairs if you collide with something.

comprehensive insurance—That which covers what the insurance companies call "acts of God and vandalism."

graduated driver's license—A license that has several stages specifying the situation under which a person can drive, ranging from supervised driving to driving with no restrictions.

Getting Ready to Drive

hybrid—A vehicle that uses at least two different power sources, such as gasoline and electricity.

hypermiling—Driving so that your car gets more miles per gallon than the EPA estimates for that car.

personal injury protection—The part of insurance that pays medical bills for you and your passengers if you are injured in a crash.

property damage liability—The part of insurance that pays for damages you cause to someone else's property.

road rage—Anger that occurs while driving in response to perceived mistakes by other drivers.

Further Reading

Gerdes, Louise I. *Teen Driving Laws*. San Diego: Greenhaven Press, 2008.

Gravelle, Karen. *The Driving Book: Everything New Drivers Need to Know but Don't Know to Ask*. New York: Walker, 2005.

Sawvel, Patty Jo. *Teen Driving*. San Diego: Greenhaven Press, 2006.

Getting Ready to Drive

Allstate—Teen Driving: Tools and Resources
<http://www.allstateteendriver.com/>

National Safety Council
<http://www.nsc.org/safety_road/TeenDriving/
Pages/teen_driving.aspx>

Teen Driving
<http://www.teendriving.com/>

Index

A

ABS brakes, 87
aggressive driving, 72, 75–76
alcohol, 68, 72–75
anatomical gift statement, 47–48
Anti-Lock Braking System, 87
attention deficit disorders, 14–15

B

bad weather driving, 62
behind-the-wheel training
  car, learning about, 30–31
  learning to see, 32–34
blind spots, 41
brain development in teens, 8–11
brakes, 87
buying cars
  factors to consider, 89–92
  financing agreements, 88–89
  insurance, 54, 79, 91, 94–99
  mechanic checks, 90
  test drive, 91–92
  used cars, 90

C

cameras, 53–55
car crashes
  color and, 97
factors involved in, 22, 57
GDL restriction effects on, 50, 52
hitting wild animals, 85
information exchange, 83
moving vehicle, 82
physical effects of, 57–59
risk factors, 57, 65, 71–72
statistics, 8, 32, 55–57, 60, 62, 67–69
car maintenance, 93
cell phones, 8, 15, 50, 63–65, 79

D

decision making, 9–10
distracted driving, 63–65
DriveCam, 54
driver education
  behind-the-wheel training (see behind-the-wheel training)
  failing, 17–19
  multitasking, 21–23
  parent-teen contracts, 36–37, 38–39
  private school, 19
  risk management, 21–23
  road test, 37–42
  rules of the road, 19–21
  simulators, 32
  teamwork approach to, 34–36

Getting Ready to Drive

traffic signs, 18, 19, 24, 41
driver's license
   anatomical gift statement,
     47–48
   appearance, color codes on,
     45–47
   commercial, 46
   documentation, 27–28
   history of, 43–44
   occupational, 46
   photos, 26–27
   police requests for, 79
   probationary/GDL restric-
     tions, 45, 46, 49–52, 68,
     80
   restrictions, 26
   suspension of, 82
   written test preparation, 23,
     24
Driver's License Agreement, 46
driver's manuals, 19–21
driving alternatives, 103
drugs, 68, 74–75
drunk driving, 68, 72–75
dyslexia, 14

E

ecodriving, 107–109
environmental impacts,
   100–102
eye movements study, 32–34

F

fatigue, 68
financing agreements, 88–89
following too closely (tailgating),
   60–62
fuel use, calculating, 105

G

getting stopped, 76–82
glasses, corrective lenses, 26
graduated driver licensing (GDL)
   restrictions, 45, 46, 49–52,
   68, 80

H

hands-free devices, 64–65
high-risk behaviors, 8, 12, 15,
   62–63, 86
hit and run, 85
hybrid cars, 109
hypermiling, 103–106

I

identification, 28
immigrants, 28
impulsivity, 15
insurance, 54, 79, 91, 94–99

L

language problems, 16
learner's permits, 16, 19,
   23–28, 51
learning disabilities, 13–16
liability insurance, 98

M

marijuana, 74
monitoring devices, 53–55
motorcycle awareness, 22
motor sports performance
   training, 85–86
multitasking, 21–23

O

oil changes, 93
organ donation, 47–48

P

parent-teen contracts, 36–37, 38–39
passengers, 52, 65, 78–79
Patriot Act, 28
payment help, 99
personal injury protection (PIP), 98
primary seat belt laws, 67
proof of citizenship, 28

Q

QuickFail, 24

R

readiness to drive
   brain development in teens, 8–11
   expectations of teens in, 11
   judging, 11–12
   learning disabilities and, 13–16
   overview, 7–8, 16
registration, 41, 79
respect, 79
risk management, 21–23
road rage, 72, 75–76
road test, 37–42
road test examiners, 37, 41

S

safety
   brakes, 87
   distractions, 63–65, 79–80
   experience, benefits of, 59–60
   facts, teen response to, 70
   fatigue, 68
following too closely (tailgating), 60–62
road conditions, accounting for, 62
scanning, 34, 66
seat belts, 22, 36, 54, 57, 60, 66–69, 76, 78
secondary seat belt laws, 67
showing hands, 78–79
simulators, 32
spatial processing, 9
speeding, 41, 62–63, 69, 79
Steer It, Clear It, 82

T

tailgating, 60–62
Teen Safe Driver, 54
Teen Unsafe Driving Behavior, 70
texting, 8, 63, 64, 79–80
three-second rule, 61–62
traffic signs, 18, 19, 24, 41

V

vehicle inspection, registration, 41, 79
vision testing, 26
visual processing disorders, 14
vocational rehabilitation programs, 16

W

"what if" strategy, 34
winter driving, 22